HOUSE
OF
GAMES

A Screenplay by
DAVID MAMET

Based on a Story by
David Mamet and Jonathan Katz

Grove Weidenfeld
New York

Published by Grove Weidenfeld
A division of Wheatland Corporation
841 Broadway
New York, NY 10003-4793

Library of Congress Cataloging-in-Publication Data

Mamet, David.
  House of games.

  I. Title.
PS3563.A4345H6   1987   791.43'72   86-32013
ISBN 0-8021-3028-3 (pbk.)

Manufactured in the United States of America

Printed on acid-free paper

First Evergreen Edition 1987

10 9 8 7 6 5 4 3 2

INTRODUCTION:
A FIRST-TIME FILM DIRECTOR

I started writing screenplays about seven years ago (*The Postman Always Rings Twice*) and, along with most other screenwriters and other ranks, conceived a desire to direct movies. My agent told me that the best way to break into that job was this: write an original screenplay and hope someone wants it badly enough to bet on you as a director.

Michael Hausman, producer of *Amadeus, Ragtime, Desert Bloom, Gregorio Cortez*, et cetera, liked the screenplay and gave me the chance to direct it, which I did.

Here are some thoughts on directing my first movie:

FAMILIAR AND NONFAMILIAR OCCUPATIONS

I once had to take a specific dose of pills with me on a trip. I shook the pills out of the bottle, counted them carefully, tore a sheet of paper out of my notebook, wrote the dose and directions on the sheet, and poured the pills onto the sheet and twisted it into a spill.

As I did this, I was overcome with a sense of *déjà vu*. "I have *absolutely* done this before," I thought. This was a feeling I never had while directing the film.

It seemed to me, prior to attempting the job, that film directing was like barn raising: the job was laid out, the opposing walls would be hoisted up, and the farmer would scramble up a ladder to peg the opposing walls together. If the farmer had not done his job correctly, he would be left fifty feet in the air, leaning against an unsupported wall, with the people who employed him and the people he employed standing down below and watching his shame.

I'd written for the movies before, worked with the directors, and been around a set. It was obvious to me that there were many aspects to the job, that I was good at some of them, competent at others, and at a complete loss in several of the most important. In those areas in which I have no talent and little understanding, it occurred to me, I had better have either a good plan or a good excuse.

The area in which I was most completely ignorant was, unfortunately, the visual. So I decided that in the absence of talent and experience, it would be good to have a plan.

I decided to plan out the whole movie, shot-by-shot, according to my understanding of the theories of Sergei Eisenstein.

I found Eisenstein's theories particularly refreshing as they didn't seem to call for any visual talent. The shot, he said, not only *need* not, but *must* not be evocative. The shot should stand as one unemotional term of a sequence, the totality of which should create in the mind of the audience a new idea, e.g., rather than the shot of a distraught woman crying, or the same woman describing to her friend over the telephone how she found out her husband was cheating on her, Eisenstein would suggest the following: (1) shot of woman reading a note; (2) shot of the note, which reads "Honey, I'll be home late tonight. Going bowling, I love you"; (3) shot of woman putting down the note, looking down at something on the floor; (4) her point of view, shot of the bowling ball in the bowling ball-bag.

In the latter example above, each of the shots is uninflected and unemotional and so the shots could be determined by someone without visual "talent," who knew the "meaning" of the sequence, i.e., a woman discovers her husband is cheating on her.

So I thought, "Well, that's for me," I'm not going to be John Ford or Akira Kurosawa, but I *do* know the meaning of each of the sequences, having written them, and if I can reduce the meaning of each of the sequences to a series of shots, each of them clean and uninflected (i.e., not necessitating further narration), then the movie will "work"; the audience will understand the story through the medium of pictures, and the movie will be as good or bad as the story I wrote.

That was the task I set myself in preparation: to reduce the script, a fairly verbal psychological thriller, to a *silent movie*. It seemed to be a tough, and possibly pointless, task, but I've always been more comfortable sinking while clutching a good theory than swimming with an ugly fact.

So I made out the shotlist, then I tried to sketch the shotlist in a bunch of cunning little rectangles each representing what the shot would look like on the screen. Then I arrived in Seattle to direct the movie.

PRE-PRODUCTION

Three people were in the production office in Seattle. Somebody went to Ambercrombie and Fitch and got their deluxe "Pigeon Shoot" dart game. We played pigeon shoot for much of the first few days. We drove around and scouted locations, I wrote letters to friends back home. "This is a breeze," I thought. Then the cast and crew showed up.

As a kid I did a lot of white-water canoeing. Once up in Michigan, I was in the stern, shooting some rapids, when we hit a bad rock broadside, and swamped. The canoe with me in it was pinned upside down in the white water, and the force of the water was such that I couldn't get out. "I'd be okay," I thought, "if someone would just turn this thing off."

Our producer had to put together "the board," that is, the schedule of what gets shot when; the production designer had questions about the color of a wall; the costume designer wanted to go out shopping; the propmaster wanted to know how many poker chips of which color were needed; the transportation captain, et cetera. Now: this was the kind of action I was looking forward to. I like to make decisions, and I like to be at the center of things, but this was a bit too much of a good thing. Everybody said that the prime requirement for a film director was good health, and I quickly saw the reason why. Each decision is important. Each decision is going to affect the film. Each choice presented to you is the result of work and thought and concern on the part of the person asking the question. Sloppiness won't do, and petulance won't do. Also, I had *prayed* for the chance to direct a movie, nothing would do but to do the job, which I was fast realizing was in the main, administrative.

So I got the job in hand and tried to remember to meditate twice a day, and preproduction was going along pretty well. Then we started with the *Real* storyboard.

The *Real* storyboard was going to be drawn by our professional storyboard artist, Jeff Ballsmeier. It was to be, in effect, a comic book of the entire movie, showing what the camera was to shoot, where the camera was to move.

Ballsmeier and I and our cinematographer, Juan Ruiz-Anchia started meeting to transform *my* storyboard into *the* storyboard.

The only trouble with my original efforts was that all my drawings looked like amoebas, and that those things they represented "would not cut."

CROSSING THE LINE

And so, as Stanislavsky would say periodically to his students: "Congratulations, you have reached the next step of your education."

The storyboard conferences were incredibly exhausting for me. I had to force myself to think in totally new concepts. Most of these concepts were on the order of "How many boxes are hidden in this pile?" and it was like taking a visual intelligence test for several hours every day, with the questions written in a foreign language.

In cutting film, the *axis* of the shot, I learned, has to be preserved. If the hero enters looking to his *left* at the heroine, then, in subsequent shots, he has to *continue* looking to his left. You can't cut to a close-up and see him looking to his *right*. *Unless* . . . and here followed a list of Talmudic exceptions which I could never follow, but which Jeff and Juan discussed quite a bit, while I felt *very* stupid.

One is not supposed to *cut-in-axis*, i.e., from a longshot of a subject to a *closer* shot of the same subject or vice versa, unless . . . et cetera.

When trying to show *passage of time*, one had better not cut from the subject to the same subject again *unless* . . .

All these rules are to this point: *don't confuse the viewer*. I tried and tried, and the editor, Trudy Ship, showed up and said don't worry, it will become clearer when you're in the editing process. The next one will be easier. (*Insh'allah*.) And so we went on making up the shotlist, the conference room was covered with diagrams, the table was covered with sketches. Juan and I and Jeff would pace and posture around the room saying things to each other like "Okay: I'm the ashtray and you're the camera," and getting very excited. It felt like the Algonquin Round Table on Speed.

My days of preproduction were like this. I would go from a costume fitting to a storyboard conference, to a location scout, and, driving back to my apartment I hit the same tree three nights in a row. I would arrive home, thank God I hadn't fallen asleep on the way, take my foot off the brake and start out of the car, and the car, which was still in drive, would proceed into the tree.

The numbers on the days-to-shoot notice on the office wall

got lower and lower. The cast showed up for rehearsal, we were all Old Cronies, and had worked together on the stage, most of us, for at least a decade, and had a happy reunion in Seattle. Rehearsals went swimmingly, and it was just about time to shoot.

Full of beans, and happy in the flush of having convinced somebody to let me direct a film, I said to myself: think past the shooting process. Plan the film, and always think toward the *editing*. The script, for good or ill, is finished, and it's going to work; you have wonderful actors, you have a superb Director of Photography, don't go out there on the set to "improvise," or even to "create," but, simply, *to stick to the plan*. If the plan is good and the script is good, the movie will cut together well and the audiences will enjoy the story. If the plan is *no* good, or the script is *no* good, then being brilliant or "inventive" on the set isn't going to be to much avail. In effect, Keep It Simple, Stupid.

Well, those were fine words, and very comforting to me, and I put up a great front and ate a lot of fresh Seattle Salmon with the cast and crew and preproduction went on apace.

Always a cocky lad, I had told the producer not to worry about me as a first-time director—that he would get either a good film or a sincere apology. The night before the first shot, my jollity came back to haunt me and I had a *crise de foi*. I couldn't sleep, I got the shakes, "I can't *do* this," I thought, "who in the *world* am I fooling?" And I wallowed in self-pity and fear for awhile, until the words of the great Dan Beard came to me: "Just because you're lost," he said, "don't think your compass is broken." And then I was, for that moment, suffused with Peace. I wasn't taxed, I saw, with having to make a masterpiece. Whether or not the movie was even any *good* was, at this point (on the night before shooting), fairly well out of my hands, all *I* had to do was stick to the plan. "Hell I can do *that*," I thought, "all I've got to be is obstinate." So I went to sleep.

THE SHOOT

We had forty-nine scenes and forty-nine days to do them in. We had to average approximately two and a half pages a day (about average). We had about twelve hours a day to get those two and a half pages.

Each day Juan and I and Christine Wilson, the script supervisor, would meet with Ned Dowd, the first assistant director (the man who ran the set), and reduce the storyboard to a list of shots, e.g., scene two: (1) a master of the entire action, (2) a close-up of the patient, (3) a close-up of Doctor Ford, (4) an insert of Ford's wristwatch, (5) a shot of Ford writing on a pad, etc.

We would plan to shoot in one direction as much as possible, so as not to have to relight twice, then turn the camera and shoot in the reverse direction. The average shotlist for each day was nine shots. And we would proceed in a deliberate and orderly fashion, cast and crew, from one shot to the next, and then go home and fall into what I wish I could describe as a dreamless sleep, but which comes closer to a "night of fitful musings." (I should point out things proceeded in an "orderly fashion" until the end of the shoot, when I, "smelling the barn," as it were, began to lose it, a bit, and wish that everything could happen all at once so I could get dressed up and go to the Opening.)

My job, once the shooting began, was a lot of worry, and a lot less work. Having started into the day's shotlist, I was fairly free from one shot to the next, and improved the hours by drinking tea, while our magnificent crew worked full out dealing with the foreseen: the necessity of putting light in places where it is not and taking it away from places where it is; and the unforeseen: cars that would not start, a mailbox that had to be removed, a prison elevator to which the key had been lost, a ruined costume, et cetera.

I was in constant awe of the crew, camera, light, and grips. Many friends and acquaintances had told me that a film director's life was taken up with the professional intransigence of the crew and time-wasting minutiae. My experience was completely the opposite. I felt that the crew were setting the example and that I was just along for the ride, and would (and did) do well to follow them. They were up all day, they were up all night, they were hanging lights on window ledges ten stories up, they spent the night in a crane in the rain.

They came over to ask me my opinion regularly, not because of any talent on my part, or because of any expertise I had demonstrated, but because the film is a hierarchy and it was my job *to do one part of it*; to provide an aesthetic overview, and to be able to express that overview in simple, practicable terms: more light on her face, *less* light on her face; the car in the background, *no* car in the background.

I came over to the camera once every hour or so to "approve" a shot the D.P. set up. My "approval" drill was this: go over to the camera, look through the lens at a brilliant, clear composition which reflected the essential nature of the shot, thank the cinematographer, return to my camper.

Most of "approving the shot" made me a bit nervous. I understood the drill of deference, I understood that *someone* had to be in charge of the movie, and that someone was me, and that I was doing it; but I *did* feel like a great big interloper looking through the camera. One part I did like was turning my hat around. I wore a beaked hat throughout the shooting, and when I walked over to the camera I would drop my glasses off my face and turn my hat around, so that I could get close to the eyepiece. That was a never-failing source of enjoyment, and I felt great and I felt I *looked* great doing it. The hat was given to me by Dorothy Jeakins, the costume designer. She designed *The Postman Always Rings Twice* (1980), which was my first experience with the movies. And she had worked with Cecil B. DeMille, and told me the hat was from some DeMille extravaganza, I have forgotten which. I also rented a pair of jodhpurs to wear on my first day as a director.

My plan was to show up on the set in jodhpurs, a monocle, and my Dorothy Jeakins hat. On the way to the set, however, this costume struck me as a tad *chudspadik*, and so I, thank goodness, refrained. (I *did* put this directing drag on after finishing the first day's shooting, and posed in it with the actors on that day, Ms. Crouse and Ms. Karen Kohlhaas, who plays the film's incarcerated murderess.)

Mike Hausman, the film's producer, thoughtfully scheduled an easy one and a half page scene as the first day's work. So we finished that scene and another two-page scene written for the same location, but scheduled for the *next* day, all in three hours and I ended my first day as a director, *one day ahead of schedule* (which was, of course, Mr. Hausman's secret plan) and I put on the jodhpurs and posed for a picture.

I didn't take too much of a deep breath until after the third day of shooting, when our first day's dailies came back from New York. I got drunk with my assistant, Mr. Zigler, and we poured ourselves from "The Thirteen Coins" restaurant into the screening room, and there, sure enough, was the film we took on the first day. Juan's photography was beautiful, the acting was beautiful, it was going to cut together and make a movie.

There's an old joke about the below-stairs gossip on the night after the Prince and the Princess got married. "What happened?" says the butler. "Well," says the chambermaid, "The Prince comes in, the Princess says: 'I offer you my honor,' the Prince replies, 'I honor your offer.' "And that's it?" says the butler, "Yep, that's about it," says the chambermaid, "all night long: honor, offer, honor, offer."

And that was about it for the shooting of the movie. Shoot, go home, shoot, go home, et cetera.

In September in New York, I was on a panel with Spike Lee, Alex Cox, Frank Perry, and Susan Seidelman. The topic of the panel was: Directors Discuss Independent Films. As questions were addressed to the other panelists, I listened and thought, enviously, "Gee, I wish *I* could be a film director." That's how it was on the set. Day by day we followed the plan. No "light at the end of the tunnel"—just getting the day's work done. At night we went to the dailies and Juan and Mike Hausman and I sat in the back row with Trudy Ship, the editor, and I would look at the takes I asked to have printed and tell Trudy my preference, and in what order the shots could be tacked together to make the scene.

At the beginning of shooting, I printed only two takes of each shot. As the shooting went on and I got more and more fatigued, I started to print more and more takes. One day Mike Hausman suggested politely (and correctly) that I was "going native," and that I only had to print one or two; and, if those were not sufficient, I could always print up the outtakes. Not only was he right economically, but, I noticed, he was right artistically.

It was very easy to choose between two takes of a shot. I found it very difficult to choose between three and impossible to choose between more. As my fatigue led to vague anxiety, I had to remind myself more frequently to Stick to the Plan and Keep It Simple, Stupid: to follow the shotlist and storyboard in such a way as to capture the simple, uninflected shots which would cut together to make the movie.

How successful is this stoical approach going to be? Well, it made the editing process very straightforward, for the most part. There were scenes which were superfluous, which had to come out; a few looks which we needed and were not shot and so had to be "stolen" from other shots or scenes, but, for the most part, the editing process, like the shooting process, was a reflection of the original plan of the storyboard.

The storyboard was, in effect, the "script" we were going out to shoot; and it is the prejudice and observation of a writer and theatergoer that, finally, the production is only as good as the script.

"FILM IS A COLLABORATIVE BUSINESS . . ."

Working as a screenwriter I always thought that the above was only half of the actual phase. From a screenwriter's point-of-view, the correct rendering should be "Film is a collaborative business: bend over."

When one works as a screenwriter, one is told that the job is analogous to being a carpenter—that as much pride and concern as one takes in one's work, one is only working for hire, and the final decision must be made by the homeowner.

The analogy, I think, is not quite correct. Working as a screenwriter-for-hire, one is in the employ *not* of the eventual consumers (the audience, whose interests the honest writer must have at heart), but of *speculators*, whose ambition is not to please the eventual consumer, but to extort from him as much money as possible. So the traditional antagonism between writer and producer is real and essential; and writers tend to deal with it by becoming enraged, leaving the business, or in the easiest way: suiting up and joining in the game by extracting as much money from the *producer* as possible.

But man oh Manischevitz what a joy to be on a project which was *not* a collaboration.

In my "Keep Printing This Shot Until Kodak Hollers Uncle" stage, I'd sit watching the dailies with ten or twenty of the cast and crew, and as I'd printed six takes and couldn't remember the first when I'd seen the sixth, I'd ask for hands on who liked which take best . . . Every time I'd ask for a vote I'd get a few giggles, a few hands, and a lot of nervousness, and then it came to me that *I* was the director, and that it wasn't funny. The people in the cast and crew were working hard enough at their job and I shouldn't, even in jest, be asking them to do mine.

"DO YOU WANT TO WORK OR DO YOU WANT TO GAMBLE?"

What did we do for fun on the set? Well, we did a whole bunch of things, and would have done more, except I am a rotten liar, and when we had planned a gag I'd be laughing so hard I couldn't say "Action," and so the object of the jokes, who was almost invariably Lindsay Crouse, would get wind that something was up.

My favorite was the Spawning Salmon. Crouse did a scene on a bench overlooking an embankment overlooking Elliott Bay. She's supposed to be staring out to sea, and we sent a production assistant down below the embankment. On cue he was to heave this ten-pound salmon up into the air, where it lands at her feet. You can see it on the Joke Reel, but Crouse is staring a few degrees off to the side, and concentrating on her acting, and she didn't actually see the salmon. Ned Dowd instructed me that good form dictated that I tell the script supervisor that we should print that take because "there was something special at the beginning that I think I liked."

Ned Dowd won fifty-six thousand dollars off of me at blackjack, and I'm just lucky that he allowed me to cut double-or-nothing One Last Time several more times. Gambling was endemic in the cast and crew. One sequence of the film is a poker game, and many of us for the week that sequence took, spent twelve hours a day in a staged poker game and the remaining twelve in a real one.

Crouse had an actor friend dress up in a bunny suit and prepared to hop through the back of a shot on her cut, but it seems that that day I was a tad "out of sorts," and so the actor stayed under the table we were shooting, dressed *en lapin* for four hours. We shot one long sequence in a poolhall, and spent a lot of time between setups shooting pool and learning trickshots from the pool hustlers, and so on, and there you have it. We were a cross between a mobile army corps, an office, and a bus-and-truck company; we were a happy family.

WHAT I REMEMBER

I remember shooting the film's last sequence on the last day of shooting. In the scene, Joe Mantegna is to get shot, and I remember his wife sitting behind the camera crying as she watched him do the various takes of his death scene.

I remember racing the dawn on a couple of weeks of night shooting; trying to get the last shot before the sun came up, and the seagulls cawing a half hour before dawn. I remember our wonderful sound man, who wanted to break into acting, and was given the part of a hotel clerk. He had to say "May I help you?" and take a pen out of a penholder and a form off of a sheaf of forms and hand them to Crouse and Mantegna. We drilled him on the specific timing of the movement of the pen and form, and told him that the whole rhythm of the shot keyed off of his precise movement; and then, on his first shot, we glued the pen into the holder and the forms together. I remember the camaraderie on the set—the sense that we were engaged together in a legitimate enterprise as part of a legitimate industry, and that hard work and dedication would ensure one a place in the profession. I remember thinking how very sad that this feeling is absent from the Theater, where *no one* is guaranteed employment from one year to the next, where this year's star writer, actor, designer, may not work again for years; and I remember feeling grateful that I could feel that camaraderie again.

WHAT I'M GOING TO DO DIFFERENTLY NEXT TIME

We finished shooting the movie on time and under budget in mid-August. I went home happy as a clam and immediately got as sick as I've ever been in my life. I couldn't get out of bed for two weeks, didn't eat a thing, and sweated the whole time. Sidney Lumet called to welcome us back. "How did the film go?" he asked my wife. She told him. "How's David," he said, "is he sick yet?"

Back in the editing room, Trudy Ship tells me that, as I look at the film, I am going to think the following three things: I shot too much, I shot too little, I shot the wrong thing. This, basically, is what I *do* think as I look at the film. There is a lot of coverage I shot that was never used; the main cost of this is not the exposed film, or even the more serious lost set-up time, but this: when capturing footage that is essential, the mood and the work on the set is, of course, more directed than when capturing footage which is protective. There is a lot I *should* have shot. There was one close-up I left out which necessitated a re-shoot and wasted a lot of worker-hours. Finally, my Master Plan was not directing the movie, *I* was directing the movie, and next time out, I'll know more about what to shoot, what not to shoot, and when to deviate from the plan.

Next time I'll eat nothing but macrobiotic food, exercise every day, and, God willing, work with exactly the same people.

D. M.

HOUSE
OF
GAMES

THE CAST

MARGARET FORD	Lindsay Crouse
MIKE	Joe Mantegna
JOEY	Mike Nussbaum
DR. LITTAUER	Lilia Skala
THE BUSINESSMAN	J. T. Walsh
GIRL WITH BOOK	Willo Hausman
PRISON WARD PATIENT	Karen Kohlhaas
BILLY HAHN	Steve Goldstein
BARTENDER/HOUSE OF GAMES	Jack Wallace
GEORGE/VEGAS MAN	Ricky Jay
POKER PLAYERS	G. Roy Levin
	Bob Lumbra
	Andy Potok
	Allen Soule
BARTENDER/CHARLIE'S TAVERN	Ben Blakeman
WESTERN UNION CLERK	Scott Zigler
SGT. MORAN	W. H. Macy
HOTEL DESK CLERK	John Pritchett
MR. DEAN	Meshach Taylor
HOTEL DOORMAN	Sugarbear Willis
GARAGE ATTENDANT	Josh Conescu
LATE STUDENT	Julie Mendenhall
STUDENT	Rachel Cline
PATIENT/FORD'S OFFICE	Patricia Wolff
MAN IN RESTAURANT	Paul Walsh
RESTAURANT HOSTESS	Roberta Maguire
WOMAN WITH LIGHTER	Jacqueline de la Chaume

THE CREDITS

Produced by	Michael Hausman
Directed by	David Mamet
Screenplay by	David Mamet

Story by	Jonathan Katz and David Mamet
Director of Photography	Juan Ruiz Anchia
Music by	Alaric Jans
Edited by	Trudy Ship
Production Designer	Michael Merritt
Costume Designer	Nan Cibula
Unit Production Manager	Lee R. Mayes
First Assistant Director	Ned Dowd
Second Assistant Director	Michael Hausman
Location Manager	Ron Lynch
Script Supervisor	Christine Wilson
Casting by	Cyrena Hausman
Production Office Coordinators	Deborah Pritchett and Cathy Sarkowsky
Assistant to the Producer	Rachel Cline
Key Production Assistant	Lynn Wegenka
First Assistant Camera	George Mooradian
Second Assistant Camera	Henry Cline
Gaffer	Michael Barrow
Best Boy	John Merriman
Key Dolly Grip	Chris Centrella
Best Boy	Hugh McCallum
Sound Mixer	John Pritchett
Boom Man	Douglas Axtell
Set Decorator	Derek Hill
Lead Man	Grey Smith
Set Dresser	Jeff Soderberg
Property Master	Samara Schaffer

MUSIC

Fugue from the Toccata in C Minor by Johann Sebastian Bach (BWV 911)
    Performed by Warren Bernhardt, piano

"This True Love Stopped for You (But Not for Me)" by Rokko Jans
    Sung by June Shellene

Fade In: Exterior: Office Building Plaza—Day

People hurrying to work across a crowded plaza. Camera moves forward toward a coffee cart in the background.

A young woman walks into the frame in the foreground. She takes a book out of her purse, looks down at the book.

Camera moves in on the book. The cover reads:

Driven
Compulsion and Obsession
in Everyday Life
by
Margaret Ford, M.D.

The book is turned over to show photo of Dr. Ford on the back cover.

> *Angle. The coffee cart, the young woman with the book in the background. Dr. Ford, taking a cup of coffee from the cart, moves toward the camera. The young woman hurries after her.*

YOUNG WOMAN: Excuse me . . . Excuse me . . .

Ford stops, the young woman comes up to her.

YOUNG WOMAN: Are you Dr. Margaret Ford . . . ?

FORD: Yes.

YOUNG WOMAN: Could I ask you, would you sign my book . . . ?

FORD: Of course.

The young woman hands the book and a pen to Ford, who signs the book.

YOUNG WOMAN: I recognized you from your picture.

FORD: Uh huh.

YOUNG WOMAN: It's the second one I've bought.

FORD: Then I am doubly pleased. Thank you for buying it. (*Ford hands the signed book back, starts to turn away.*)

YOUNG WOMAN: You've helped me very much.

FORD: I'm glad I have. (*Beat.*) Thank you. (*Beat.*) Goodbye.

Ford walks away, through the crowded plaza.

Interior: Hospital Cell—Day

  Insert—Ford's hand, writing on a pad.

WOMAN PATIENT (*voice over*): . . . and he said that we all try to run from experience. From Experience. Do you understand me . . . but that it will seek us out. Do you think that you're exempt . . . ?

  Angle—Close-up. The woman patient. Dressed in a hospital gown.

WOMAN PATIENT: I'm *talking* to you. Do you think that you're exempt?

  Angle. Ford and the woman patient, sitting across from each other in front of a white background. Ford looks up from her writing.

FORD: Do I think that I'm exempt . . . that I'm exempt from what . . . ?

WOMAN PATIENT: *Experience.*

FORD: No. I don't think I'm exempt.

WOMAN PATIENT: Well, you'd better be assured you're not.

FORD: What is the animal?

WOMAN PATIENT: The animal?

FORD: You said in your dream you saw an animal. (*Beat. Ford glances at her watch.*)

WOMAN PATIENT: It's . . .

   Angle—Insert. Ford writing on the pad.

WOMAN PATIENT (*voice over*): It's . . . I . . . I want to say . . . I don't know how to say it . . .

Interior: Greenhousey Restaurant—Day

Dr. Maria Littauer, a woman in her sixties, sitting alone at a table. Ford hurries in. Sits.

FORD: I'm so sorry I'm late.

MARIA: Oh. It's alright.

Ford sits, opens her notebook, reads.

FORD: Listen to this: in her dream: she saw a foreign animal. What is the animal? She cannot think of the name. It's saying, the animal is saying "I am only trying to do good." I say, "What name comes up when you think of this animal?" She says it is a "lurg," it is called a "lurg." So if we invert "Lurg," a "lurg" is a "girl," and *she* is the animal, and *she* is saying "I am only trying to do good."

MARIA: And now someone has heard her. Good, Maggie, good for you. And now what are you going to eat?

Maria hands Ford a menu, Ford puts it down.

FORD: I don't have time. (*Ford takes out a pack of cigarettes. Picks up a lighter from the table in front of Maria.*)

Angle—Insert. Ford, holding the gold lighter, lights her cigarette.

FORD (*voice over*): It's so beautiful. It's old and it's heavy, and it looks like someone gave it to you. Sometimes I think the only pressures in my life . . .

Angle. Maria.

MARIA: The only . . . ?

Angle.

FORD: I'm sorry . . . ?

MARIA: You said the only "pressures . . ."

FORD: "Pleasures." I said "pleasures."

MARIA: No, what you said was "pressures," you see? And this is what I'm telling you. Your book is a best seller, your income jumps up, people look at you differently, perhaps. This is confusing. Listen to me: Slow Down. Give *yourself* all those rewards you would like to have. You see a beautiful gold lighter, *buy* one for yourself. Your friend asks you to lunch, go and *eat* lunch with her.

Beat.

FORD: Do you forgive me . . . ?

MARIA (*smiles*): No. Go. Work.

Ford smiles at Maria, gets up from the table.

Interior: Ford's Office—Day

Insert. Ford's hand holding a pen. Poised to write.

MAN'S (BILLY HAHN'S) VOICE (*voice over*): a, uh . . . a . . . a
. . . I don't know . . .

The hand relaxes.

*Angle. Ford's office. She is seated across from a young man
of about thirty (Billy Hahn).*

FORD (*pause*): A what?

BILLY (*sighs*): A feeling of . . . of . . . of . . . of *nothingness.*

FORD: What does that make you think of?

BILLY (*standing, shouting*): Will you leave me *alone* . . . for
chrissake . . . what does it matter? What does it *mean*? You
understand? It's in my head or *not* . . . it doesn't make . . .
it . . .

FORD: Billy . . .

BILLY: What? Are you going to tell me I'm "entitled to my feel-
ings . . ."? What does it . . . what. the. hell. does. it. *matter*?
(*Pause.*)

FORD: It matters if you're going to cure yourself.

BILLY: If I'm going to cure myself. And what do I do now?

FORD: What do you do now? You . . .

BILLY: No, no, what do I do today? What do I do *tomorrow*?

FORD: Today and tomorrow you say this: "I am a compulsive gambler. The reasons for this . . ."

BILLY: Oh, maan . . . oh, maan . . . *I* don't know . . . what am I *doing* here . . . ? What am I *doing* here . . . ?

FORD: You're here to take control of your life.

BILLY: I lost, what do *you* care maan, you're rich, you're comfortable, you got your goddamn *book* you wrote, you don't do *dick*, you don't do *nothing*, maan, it's all a con game, you do nothing. You say you want to help? You want to *help* . . . ? help me with *this*. (*He produces a small, nickeled automatic pistol.*) Help me with this, if you can, cause if not I got to use it.

FORD: To use it for what . . . ?

Beat.

BILLY: Aren't you going to ask me is it loaded?

FORD: To use it for what?

BILLY: To use it to *kill* myself, or, *you* know, *I* don't know, to . . .

FORD: Why would you want to kill yourself?

BILLY: What do you think this is? Some "dream"? Maan, *you're* living in the dream, your "questions," 'cause there. is. a. real. world. (*Pause.*)

FORD: And what happened to you in that world? (*Pause.*) What happened to you?

BILLY: What difference does it make? You say you "want to help." You *can't* help, 'cause, babe, you don't know what trouble *is*.

FORD: Give me the gun and I will help you. (*Pause.*) Billy. (*Pause.*) I swear to you. (*Pause.*) You give me the gun and I will help you.

He hands her the gun.

BILLY: I just lost twenty-five thousand dollars. That I do not have. And if I do not pay it by tomorrow they are going to kill me. Now: what kind of help is your damn promise now?

Interior: Ford's Office—Later—Night

Insert. Ford writing on a sheet of paper: "Compulsive succeeds in establishing a situation where he is out of control."

Angle. Ford, alone at her desk, with a cup of coffee. Smoking. Writing (pause), she sighs. Looks up, takes off her glasses. Shakes her head from side to side. She picks up off her desk Billy's nickeled automatic pistol.

Angle—Insert. The pistol in her hand. She lays it on the desk. Camera Follows her hands. She picks up a sheaf of notes, shuffles through the notes. Brings up a sheet from the bottom. On it is written: ". . . The character of Mike—the 'Unbeatable Gambler.' Seen as omniscient, who 'doles out punishment' . . . HOUSE OF GAMES.

Interior: Rundown Commercial Building—Night

A dark, dirty corridor in an old building. A woman in jeans and a leather bomber jacket walks into the frame. We see her from the back as she starts down the corridor. At the end of the corridor, she stops before a door. Looks up at the sign over the door.

Angle. It is Ford, looking at the sign. We see the sign reads:

The House of Games
Backgammon, Chess, Ping-Pong, Pool

She looks down, opens the door. She walks through the door. Camera follows her into a large hall. There are two Ping-Pong tables. A pool table. Along the side of the hall various small card tables. At one table two old men are playing gin. A Ping-Pong game is in progress. A man sits behind the cash desk. Looks at Ford. Ford takes out a cigarette. Puts it in her mouth.

MAN: N'I help you?

FORD: Yeah. I need a match.

He hands her a match. She lights her cigarette. Bob gestures at the game area.

BOB: You lookin' f'ra *partner*. To *play* something?

FORD: I'm looking for *Mike*.

BOB: Who's Mike?

FORD: Would you get him for me?

BOB: I don't think that Mike's here.

FORD: Why don't you take a look?

(Pause.) Bob shrugs. Gets up off his stool, walks to a door behind him, opens it. We hear sounds of a card game in the room behind.

Angle—Point of view. Bob beckons a man over to him. They talk in the doorway. Bob gestures at Ford. The man looks at her, starts over to her.

Angle. The other man (Mike) walks over to Ford.

MIKE: What the fuck is it?

FORD: I'm looking for Mike.

MIKE: Mike isn't here. What do you want? (*Pause.*)

FORD: A *friend* of mine . . .

MIKE: Cut to the chase, I'm very busy, what do you want with *Mike* . . .

FORD: I'm *telling* you, and *you're* Mike, and I want you to *listen* to this, 'cause you threatened to kill a *friend* of mine . . .

MIKE: Is that what I did?

FORD: Yes. That's *exactly* what you did. And I'm putting you on notice, "Mike," that that behavior doesn't go. Whether you mean it or *not*, and, it's irrelevant to *me*, because you aren't going to *do* it. Now: this is a sick kid. He's a compulsive gambler, and he hasn't got . . .

MIKE: . . . wait wait wait. What is this, what are you going to *do* to me, what are you "fronting *off*" about? And if I'm this bad dude whyn't I just take out some gun, blow you to a billion parts?

FORD: I'll tell you why. Because I think you're just a bully . . .

MIKE: Just a "bully." What, and you're not going to let me carry your *books*? Aren't *you* a caution . . .

FORD: Let's talk turkey, Pal. One: You threatened to kill my friend. You aren't going to *do* that because if you do you're going away for Life. Two is the *money*.

MIKE: Money.

FORD: Now: he doesn't *have* it, but we can . . .

MIKE: Who *is* this friend?

FORD: Billy Hahn.

MIKE: Billy Hahn. And he lost how much to me?

FORD: Come on, come on: twenty-five thousand dollars.

MIKE: Twenty-five thousand dollars Billy Hahn lost to me. Excuse me one moment, will you . . . ?

Mike walks back into the back room.

(Off camera; sotto:) Deal me out. I'll be right back . . .

Mike comes back into the room with a small briefcase, opens it up, takes out a pocket notebook.

I'm showing you this because I *like* you, okay? 'Cause you got blond hair.

He opens book. Turns to a page.

> *Angle—Insert. The page. The name "Billy Hahn," with various figures in hundreds added to, subtracted from, crossed out, the final figure is "$800.00."*

> *Angle. Ford holding the book.*

MIKE: Okay? Billy Hahn owes me eight hundred bucks.

A CARD PLAYER (*voice over*): In or Out?

MIKE (*to card player*): Out. (*To Ford:*) How come you *made* me so quick, I'm not a hard guy? How did you size me up so quick?

FORD: I, *I* don't know . . . in my work . . .

MIKE: What work is *that*?

FORD: Well, it's none of your *business* . . .

MIKE: Stand *corrected*. Here's the thing. Listen: I want something from you.

FORD: What do you want?

MIKE: I want you to do me a favor. And if you do I'll wipe out the eight hundred your friend owes me.

FORD: What do you want?

Mike draws her aside.

MIKE: Do you know what a "tell" is?

FORD: A "tell"?

He takes a coin out of his pocket.

MIKE: Here: do this:

He puts the coin in his hands, puts his hands behind his back, brings the hands in front of him.

You have to choose a hand . . . (*He hands her the coin.*) You do it to me. Do it.

She does it, brings the two hands, one of which hides the coin, in front of her. He taps one of her hands.

   Angle. She opens the hand he has tapped. It holds the coin.

   Angle. Mike and Ford.

Do it again.

She does it again, the hand he taps holds the coin.

Okay, now I can do that all day. How? You got a "tell." You're "telling" me the hand that has the coin.

FORD: I *am*?

MIKE: Yes.

FORD: How?

MIKE: It's not important. Ah, okay—you're doing it with your nose. You're pointing your nose slightly at the hand that has the coin. Okay? That's a "tell." Now: the guy from *Vegas* (*he points at the back room*) has got a shitload of my money. *He's* got a "tell." Okay? When he's *bluffing*, okay, he plays with his little gold ring. Now: I *caught* him doing it. N'he knows I did, so he *stopped*. He's conscious of himself. I want you to do me this *favor*. I want you to be my "girlfriend" for a while, come in the game, you stand *behind* me, watch me *play*. We get in a big *hand*, okay? I, uh, I go to go "pee" you *watch* this guy, and *tell* me, does he play with his gold ring. I know he's *bluffing*, I win the big hand. I'll forget the eight hundred dollars your friend owes.

FORD: If you're such a hot gambler, how'd you fall into this bind?

MIKE: Who told you I was a good gambler? I'm not a gambler, this is a *sickness* . . .

FORD: You're *not* a gambler.

MIKE: No.

FORD: Well . . . what *are* you, then?

MIKE: Aha.

Interior: Back Room—Night

Five men playing cards.

VEGAS MAN: Up two hundred.

ANDY: Your two and five more.

MIKE: I'm out.

He throws in his cards. The game continues. He leans back to talk to Ford.

MIKE: Guy's got a full house, you got two pair, it puts you in a philosophically indefensible position.

AL: New Hand.

MIKE: Well, it's good that I can *joke* about it, isn't it . . . ?

VEGAS MAN: Full house. (*He lays down his cards.*)

MIKE: What did you do, "win" again . . . ?

VEGAS MAN: That's right. You want to win the hand, you have to stay in 'til the end.

MIKE: Thank you.

   Angle—Close-up. Mike and Ford.

MIKE (*sotto*): You going to back me up here?

FORD (*sotto*): Yes.

MIKE (*sotto*): You keep looking for the tell, I'm going to *gut* that sonofabitch . . .

   Angle. Interior cardroom. Later.

MIKE: I bet the fifty.

AL: Your fifty, and one fifty back.

VEGAS MAN: Two hundred. I call it.

ANDY (*dealer*): Cards to the players. Two good players. Mike?

MIKE: One card.

A card is dealt to Mike.

Angle—Insert. He takes the card, puts it in his hand, he holds three aces.

ANDY (*voice over*): Al . . . ?

AL (*voice over*): Two cards.

VEGAS MAN (*voice over*): One card.

Angle: The card table.

MIKE: I pass.

AL: Wha's the pot? Two, four, five, *eight* hundred dollars. That's my bet.

VEGAS MAN: I call.

MIKE: You "call . . ." you only "call . . ."? Well, let's go visit Mr. More. Your eight, and I raise you twenty-five hundred dollars.

AL (*throwing in his hand*): I can't stand it. South.

VEGAS MAN: South Street Seaport the man says. He Can't Stand the Heat. He can't stand it.

MIKE: You want to play cards? The bet is two and a half thou.

VEGAS MAN: The bet? *I'll* tell you what the bet is. Your twenty-five, and I raise you six thousand bucks.

Mike pushes his chair back from the table, gets up.

MIKE: You sonofabitch, you've been steamrolling over me all night, what are you trying to tell me, one card, you caught a flush, a boat, what? I think you're bluffing pal, I think you're trying to *buy* it.

VEGAS MAN: Then you're going to have to give me some Respect, or give me some Money.

ANDY: The bet is six thousand dollars.

MIKE: I know what the goddamn bet is. I'm going to pee. (*To Ford, as he exits:*) I thought that you were going to bring me luck.

VEGAS MAN: Make your own luck.

Mike exits. Beat.

ANDY: Yes, yes, yes. Some people say *one* thing, some people say something *else*.

VEGAS MAN: The man can't *play*, he should stay *away*.

AL: His money's as good as yours is.

VEGAS MAN: His money is, and now we're going to see about his cards. That's right, Miss, isn't it?

From the back of the room, Joey, a man in his sixties, dressed like a college professor, comes forward.

JOEY: Leave the woman alone.

VEGAS MAN: I'm just making conversation. That's right, isn't it? How's he doing, Miss, you bringing him "good fortune"?

FORD: Excuse me?

VEGAS MAN: Who do you *like* here, your friend or me?

FORD: Well, I've seen his hand, but I haven't seen yours.

VEGAS MAN: That's right. That's absolutely right.

The Vegas man starts playing with his little gold ring.

Angle. Ford looking at him.

Angle—Point of view. The Vegas man turning his gold ring.

Angle. Ford, as she watches the Vegas man playing with his ring. She looks around as Mike comes back into the room.

MIKE (*voice over*): Okay.

Angle: He slides back into his seat.

Let's play some fucken *cards* . . . Now: the bet is *what* . . . ?

ANDY: You're raised six thousand dollars, Mike.

FORD: How you doing? You ready to take this guy's money . . . ?

She takes his head in her hands as if to kiss him.

Angle—Close-up. The two of them, heads together. She whispers to him.

FORD: He's bluffing.

MIKE: You saw him?

FORD: He did exactly what you said. He played with his ring, and . . .

MIKE: He did . . . ?

FORD: He's bluffing.

MIKE: Well, he *better* be, 'cause my problem is that I don't have the six. If I *lose*, I can't . . .

FORD: You aren't *going* to. He played with his ring. Call the bet.

He pulls back and looks at her a moment. He nods.

MIKE (*to Vegas man*): Six thousand dollars? (*Pause.*) I think you're *bluffing*.

VEGAS MAN: What are you, Joe *Hep*? Raise, call, or fold . . .

MIKE: I should raise your ass, but I'm just going to call. (*Generally: to the table:*) My marker's good for a moment?

VEGAS MAN: What is this "marker"? Where are you "from"?

MIKE: Where am I "from"? I'm from the United States of kiss my *ass*. My marker's *good*.

VEGAS MAN: Fuck *you*. And get the money up, or fold the goddamn *hand*.

JOEY: Look, mister: this man is a man of his word. He's a *regular* in the games—and if he says . . .

VEGAS MAN: Where I come from, the rule is if you can't call the bet you're out of the hand.

FORD: I'll call the bet.

VEGAS MAN: With what. . . ?

FORD: I said I'll back it up. If he loses I'll write you a check.

VEGAS MAN (*pause; generally*): Who is this broad?

JOEY: She's a friend of Mike's, she's alright. Your bet is called.

MIKE: Trip tens. *Beat* 'em, my friend.

The Vegas man turns over his cards.

Angle—Insert. The Vegas man has a club Flush. Pause.

Angle. The table full of men, looking at the hand.

VEGAS MAN: All blue. (*To Ford:*) You owe me six thousand dollars. (*He stands and starts raking in his chips.*) Thank you very *much*, next case.

The Vegas man and the others move away.

ANDY (*over his shoulder*): Tough beat, Mike . . .

Mike and Ford are left alone at the table.

MIKE: Huh. (*Mike gets up, stunned; takes Ford over in the corner.*) Huh. (*Pause.*)

JOEY: Tough beat, Mike.

MIKE: I, uh . . . (*He shakes his head.*) He didn't do the thing with his ring.

FORD (*nods head*): No, he *did* it.

MIKE: He *did*, n'a-*fuck* is he doing with a Flush. . . ? (*To Vegas man:*) What the *fuck* are you doing with a *Flush*?

VEGAS MAN: Does that beat trips in Chicago? (*Pause.*) Well, then. Gimme the goddamn money.

MIKE (*to Ford*): We lost.

FORD: I have gathered that.

VEGAS MAN: And if you think I'm leaving here without that check, you're out of your motherfucking mind.

MIKE: *Okay. Okay*, hey, don't get Pushy.

VEGAS MAN: Pushy, Jim . . . ? Pushy . . . ? You don't know what pushy *is*.

He takes a large pistol out of his back pocket, puts it on the table.

Now give me my six thousand dollars.

Beat.

MIKE (*to Ford*): Uh, look, I'm going to have to ask you for that money.

FORD: That's right.

MIKE: I can't tell you how *sorry* I am . . .

FORD: No, no, *please*: let's just complete this transaction, and . . .

She starts writing check.

MIKE: I think that's probably wise . . .

VEGAS MAN: . . . and this check had better be like gold, or I'm coming back here, because I *won* this money.

MIKE: Okay, okay. You're going to get your money . . .

Angle—Insert. Ford's hand writing the check, beyond it, the revolver of the Vegas man.

Angle—Close-up. Ford, looking intently at something.

Angle—Point of view. Very tight on the revolver, the muzzle end is leaking little drops of water.

Angle. Ford, surrounded by the men at the table. She stops writing.

FORD: You know what? I don't think I'm going to pay you.

JOEY: *Don't* get the guy mad . . . for *heaven's* sake: *don't* get the guy *mad* . . .

MIKE: *Pay* the man.

VEGAS MAN: You crazy bitch. Pay me what you *owe* . . .

He picks up the revolver. The other men retreat.

FORD: No. I don't think I will (*she folds up the check and drops it in her purse*), and I will *tell* you why not: is that *you cannot threaten someone with a Squirtgun!*

VEGAS MAN: You crazy bitch, I can threaten you with anything I goddamn want.

MIKE: George.

VEGAS MAN: Shuddup.

MIKE: George.

VEGAS MAN: What?

MIKE: I think it's Olley Olley In Free.

VEGAS MAN: No, I'm doing fine.

JOEY: No, George, you've blown the Gaff.

VEGAS MAN: I have?

MIKE: Yes.

VEGAS MAN: I told you a squirtgun wouldn't work.

MIKE: A squirtgun would've worked. You didn't have to *fill* it.

VEGAS MAN: What, am I going to threaten someone with an empty gun . . . ?

MIKE: No, George, you're right, of course.

FORD: You guys are fantastic. What do you, do this for a living . . . ?

VEGAS MAN: Ask her is she mad.

MIKE: You aren't miffed with us, are you, I mean, nothing personal.

FORD: You were going to con me out of my money.

MIKE: It was only business.

FORD: It was only business, huh?

JOEY: It's the American Way. I don't know about the rest of you, but I'm starved. Anyone care for a snack . . . ?

Joey leaves the room, followed by the Vegas man.

VEGAS MAN: I told you a damn squirtgun wouldn't work.

JOEY: (*sotto*): One-eyed Jacks, Man with the Ax, suicide King.

Beat. Ford is alone with Mike.

MIKE: Well, there you have it.

FORD: A sucker born every minute, huh?

MIKE: And two to take him. Play past it. Here: (*He picks up a House of Games chip.*) A souvenir of your close escape from con men.

Beat. Ford laughs, takes the chip.

Exterior: House of Games—Night

Ford, Vegas man, Mike and Joey, lounging around, eating hot-dogs, at an open-air market, across from the House of Games.

MIKE (*to Joey*): Oh! Tell her the Mitt.

JOEY: Na, they're still *using* the Mitt today, show her something historical . . .

VEGAS MAN: Show her the Tap.

MIKE: What, they aren't doing the Tap. It's like a *kid's* game.

JOEY (*to Ford*): Okay. You run a candy store. Miss, excuse me, please, I'd like that Spearmint Gum. (*He digs for a bill; hands it to her.*) You say, "Don't you have anything smaller?"

FORD: Don't you have anything smaller.

JOEY: No, I'm *sorry* . . . you make change . . . give me the change . . .

MIKE: *George*, what the *hell* are you doing out of the office . . . ?

JOEY: . . . I . . . (*To Ford:*) Okay? I pick up the ten bucks change. I leave the ten. I leave the gum. (*To Mike:*) I'm on my lunch hour.

MIKE: I'm gonna have your job, you *know* that? I'm going to *Anderson* . . .

JOEY (*to Ford*): Oh. I found a nickel . . . I'm sorry . . . I hand you the nickel and I take back the ten and the gum. Timing, timing, it's all timing!

MIKE: Gum is not a nickel anymore.

JOEY: Shows you how long since I did the . . .

VEGAS MAN: Here's your cab.

Mike gets up, starts to walk her to the cab.

FORD: Gentlemen, good evening.

Camera follows them as they walk. She turns back.

My friend's square with you. On the eight hundred dollars.

MIKE: Well, I *thought* you'd probably say that.

FORD: We struck the bargain. You said, "Watch for the tell and you'd cancel his debt." A man of your word?

MIKE: Alright. He's square.

FORD: May I have the I.O.U.?

MIKE: Hey, you're right—what's right is right. (*He hands her the I.O.U.*) Come back again and I'll show you some other Jolly Pranks.

FORD: Thank you.

Camera follows them to the cab. The cab is waiting at the curb. Mike knocks on the window, the cabbie opens the door.

(*To Ford:*) Who are you, by the way?

FORD: Thank you for a lovely evening.

MIKE: You're a lovely woman. Come back any time you'd enjoy some more excitement.

She gets in the cab. Cab starts to drive away.

  Angle. Mike watching the cab drive away. He reaches in his pocket, takes out a coin.

Angle—Insert. Mike manipulating the coin. A half dollar. He puts the coin in one palm, rubs his hands together, opens one hand at a time, the coin is gone.

Angle. Mike, still watching the cab. He puts his hand to his mouth, coughs. Opens his hand, which now holds the coin, flips the coin into the air. Looks at the departing cab.

Angle—Point of view. The cab turning a corner down the street. It is gone.

Angle. Mike. Flips the coin up again. Catches it, puts it in his pocket, turns and starts back into the building.

Interior: Ford's Apartment—Night

A picture window, Lake Michigan beyond it. Curtains blowing. Classical music playing. Ford, dressed in a chaste flannel nightgown, carrying a cup of tea, walks into the frame, closes the window. Camera follows her around the apartment. Obviously the abode of a single woman. Small, neat, modern, non-personal. She goes into the kitchen. Finishes her tea, puts the cup in the sink. Turns off the radio. Turns off the lights in the living room. She goes into the bedroom, turns down the covers on her bed. Gets into the bed. Pause. Picks up the House of Games chip from the bedside table, looks at it. She gives a big belly laugh, laughs for a moment. Turns out the lights, snuggles down into the bed.

Interior: Hospital—Day

A window. A hospital-gowned woman patient, smoking a cigarette, walks into the frame.

WOMAN PATIENT: He said, "I can make any woman a whore in fifteen minutes."

FORD (*off camera*): . . . and what did you say to that?

WOMAN PATIENT: I said he couldn't make anybody a whore that was not a whore to start out with.

The woman nods, as if agreeing with herself.

Angle. The hospital room. The woman patient packing. Ford, seated, talking to her.

He said, "I been reading your mail, and you *are* that whore." And . . . (*pause*) *later* you see . . . (*Pause.*) When . . . then . . . then . . . 'cause he didn't realize what he had done.

FORD: And what *had* he done . . . ?

WOMAN PATIENT: You know, I know there are people who are normal . . .

FORD: *Are* there?

WOMAN PATIENT: Yes, there are. But . . .

FORD: But what?

WOMAN PATIENT: But I don't know what those people . . . *do* . . .

Pause. The woman starts to cry. Pause. Ford goes over to her.

It's alright, darling . . .

WOMAN PATIENT: No. It's not alright. It never was alright. How can you live, when you've done something . . . when . . . ?

Interior: Hospital Corridor, Prison Ward—Day

Ford walking down the corridor, escorted by a policeman. He escorts her through a locked door.

Maria comes around the corner.

FORD (*to Maria*): I have to talk to you.

Exterior: Hospital—Day

Ford and Maria sitting on a bench, the hospital in the background.

FORD: Why do we listen to their troubles when we can't help them?

MARIA: Oh. You have been talking to your murderess again.

FORD: I know why she is in the hospital, she's sick. The question is what am *I* doing there. It's a sham, it's a con game. There's nothing I can do to help her, and there's nothing I can learn from her to help others avoid her mistakes. That poor girl, all her life my father tells her she's a whore, so all her life she seeks out . . .

MARIA: "My father . . ."?

FORD: I'm sorry?

MARIA: You said, "*My* father says that she's a whore."

FORD: *My* father . . . ? (*Beat.*) I said, "*My*" father . . . ?

MARIA: Take your own prescription. If you're driven to do a thing you don't like, do something *else*. What gives you satisfaction? (*Pause.*) Maggie: what gives you satisfaction, what do you always enjoy?

FORD: I . . . I don't know . . . I enjoyed writing my *book* . . .

MARIA: So write another book. And in the short term, you come to my house for dinner tonight, will you do that?

Ford takes out her appointment book. Beat.

FORD: I'm sorry, I can't come tonight.

MARIA: Tonight, excuse me for asking, you have something to do that brings you joy?

FORD: Yes. I think I do.

Beat.

MARIA: Good. That's good.

Maria gets up, leaving Ford alone on the bench. Ford looks at her appointment book.

> *Angle—Point of view. The check made out for six thousand dollars, clipped into the book.*

Exterior: House of Games—Night

Ford, dressed in casual clothes, walking across the street to the House of Games. She passes Bob, the proprietor.

BOB: You come back to play some pool?

FORD: I'm looking for Mike.

BOB: Mike ain't here, try down at Charlie's.

FORD: Thanks.

Angle. Ford walking across the street, takes out a cigarette, lights it. Camera follows her around the corner. In the middle of the block is a "lounge" with a large neon sign "Charlie's." Ford brushes back her hair, flicks away her cigarette, walks into the lounge.

Interior: Charlie's—Night

A dark lounge. Men and a couple of women at the bar watching a sports event on television. Ford is walking slowly past the bar, looking around.

BARTENDER: . . . help you?

She shakes her head "no." Looks around again.

. . . drinking?

FORD: Scotch and water.

She points to an empty booth. The bartender nods. Ford goes over to the booth and slides in. Looks around again. She lights another cigarette. Beat.

A waiter, seen only from the waist down, napkin over his arm, comes into the frame.

WAITER: Scotch and water.

FORD (*without looking up*): Thank you.

WAITER: You pay now.

FORD (*opens her purse*): How much is it?

WAITER: How much have you got?

Ford looks up.

   Angle. The waiter is Mike, dressed in a good suit, who has just draped a napkin over his arm. Mike slides into the booth.

MIKE: Oldest trick in the book. Never fails. Not *good* for much of anything, but still of great historical interest. Hiya.

FORD: Hi.

MIKE: Did I ever tell you my name? My name is Mike.

FORD: Glad to meet you. I've got a *proposition* for you.

MIKE: And what's "your" name?

FORD: Listen to this: how would you feel if someone were to do a *study* of . . . a study of . . . the *confidence* game . . . and someone were to *talk* to you, and learn your views and watch the way you operate. (*Pause.*)

MIKE: "A study of." (*Pause.*)

FORD: Yes.

MIKE: For what?

FORD: For my own reasons.

MIKE: And that's why you came back here?

FORD: Yes . . . how would you feel about that?

MIKE: Is that what you want? To see how a true bad man plies his trade . . . ?

FORD: Yes. (*Beat.*)

MIKE: Alright. (*He gets up and extends his hand to her.*)

Exterior: City Street—Night

Ford and Mike walking.

MIKE: The basic idea is this: it's called a *"confidence"* game. Why? Because you give me your confidence? No. Because I give you *mine.* So what we have here, in addition to "Adventures in Human Misery," is a short course in psychology. How do you get money when you *have* no money? (*He indicates with his head that they are to enter a building.*) This is called "Short Con." Watch closely.

> *Angle—Point of view. They are entering an all-night Western Union office.*

Interior: Western Union Office—Night

Ford and Mike sitting in the empty office, reading old magazines. Pause. A young man enters the office. As he does so Mike gets up and goes over to the cashier's window.

MIKE (*to cashier*): Would you please check *again*, please. Howard. Martin *Howard* . . . money order for three hundred . . .

CLERK: It hasn't come *in* yet. As I told you, sir, the moment . . .

MIKE: . . . it was supposed to have been here this aft . . .

CLERK: . . . the *moment* it . . .

MIKE: . . . alright. Alright. Thank you.

Mike goes back and sits down. The young man goes up to the window.

YOUNG MAN (*to cashier*): I'm expecting some money? John Moran . . . ?

CASHIER: One moment. (*He checks.*) Moran . . . ?

YOUNG MAN: Yessir.

CASHIER: No, I'm sorry. It hasn't . . .

YOUNG MAN: They told me definitely by nine o'. . .

CASHIER: If you'll have a seat I'll tell you the *moment* . . .

YOUNG MAN: Thank you.

He sits down, across from Ford and Mike. Pause. Mike sighs.

MIKE: Can you beat that? (*Pause.*) Can you beat this? I've been waiting here since . . . (*To Ford:*) Honey. . . ? (*To young man:*) Since three o'clock this afternoon.

YOUNG MAN: No.

MIKE: Three o'clock this afternoon. I got my *car* stolen, my *wallet* . . . kid in a hotel, he hasn't *eaten* since . . .

YOUNG MAN: They told me they'd have my money by *nine*, and . . .

MIKE: I swear to god . . .

YOUNG MAN: . . . and I've got to get a *bus* ticket before . . .

MIKE: . . . when does the bus leave?

YOUNG MAN: . . . not til six. But it's selling out, and I've got to pick the ticket up by . . .

MIKE: . . . where you going?

YOUNG MAN: . . . back to Camp.

MIKE: . . . where is that?

YOUNG MAN: Pendleton.

MIKE: You're in the Corps? *I* was in the Corps.

YOUNG MAN: When were you in?

MIKE: '69, '70—yeah, *I* was there . . .

YOUNG MAN (*extending his hand*): John Moran.

MIKE: John. Marty Howard. (*Shakes hand. Pause.*) *Okay.* Look. What do you need for the bus?

YOUNG MAN: Forty.

MIKE: When my money comes in I'll give you the forty. Go back to the . . .

YOUNG MAN: No, I couldn't take it.

MIKE: The *Hell.* What are you going to? Miss your Formation? I'll lend you the forty. When you get back to Pendleton, send it back. (*Pause.*)

YOUNG MAN: Um.

MIKE: No. You get on that bus.

YOUNG MAN: *Thank* you.

MIKE: Nothing to it.

YOUNG MAN: If *mine* comes in first . . .

MIKE: No, *we'll* be alright . . .

YOUNG MAN: Uh uh. No. If *mine* comes in first *you* take . . .

MIKE: No. I couldn't do that . . .

CASHIER: *Moran* . . . ?

The young man goes over to the window.

Could I see some I.D., please . . . ?

YOUNG MAN (*to Mike*): Now: you've got to take . . . what do you need?

MIKE: No. *We'll* get by . . .

YOUNG MAN (*turns around with money in his hands*): No. You tell me: what do you need . . . ?

Mike gestures to the soldier with the money in his hand.

MIKE (*to Ford*): What's more fun than human nature!? (*He takes Ford by the hand and starts out the door. To the soldier:*) Save your money, Pally. *Semper Fi* . . .

Exterior: Western Union Office—Night

Ford and Mike exiting the office.

FORD: Well. You learn something new every day.

MIKE: Innit the truth? You impressed?

FORD: So "you can't cheat an Honest Man."

MIKE: That's probably true. But what we have just seen is the operation of a slightly different philosophic principle.

FORD: Which is?

MIKE: "Don't Trust Nobody." Also this: everybody gets something out of every transaction. What that nice kid gets is the opportunity to feel like a good man. (*Pause.*) Now: what do *you* get out of *this* transaction?

FORD: I told you, I . . .

MIKE: Be *real*, Babe. Let's up the ante here. (*He stops.*) Do you want to make love to me . . . ?

FORD: *Excuse* me . . . ?

MIKE: Because you're blushing. *That's* a tell. The things we want, we can do them or not do them, but we can't hide them.

FORD: And *what* is it you think I want?

MIKE: I'll tell you: someone to come along, to take you into a new thing. Do you want that? Would you like that?

Beat.

FORD (*softly*): Yes.

MIKE: *What* is it . . . ?

FORD: Yes.

MIKE: That's good.

Interior: Hotel Lobby—Night

Ford and Mike walking through the lobby of a very fine hotel. Many people in the lobby. Camera follows them up to the check-in desk.

MIKE (*to clerk*): A room.

CLERK (*checking files*): Your name, sir?

MIKE (*as he takes out some cash*): Douglas Johnson.

CLERK (*checking files*): I'm . . . you have a reservation . . . ?

MIKE: No, I . . .

CLERK: Oh, I'm *so* sorry, Mr. Johnson, we're *completely* booked up with the Apparel Show . . .

As the clerk talks, a well-built black man in a tuxedo drops his key off on the desk.

WELL-BUILT BLACK MAN: Goodnight.

CLERK (*to black man*): Goodnight, Mr. Dean.

MIKE: Well . . .

CLERK (*to Mike*): I'm very sorry, sir . . .

MIKE (*pointing, behind desk*): Who's that man? Is that the manager?

The clerk turns to see who Mike is pointing at.

   Angle. Mike's hand on the counter. Picks up the key that Mr. Dean has just left off.

CLERK (*voice over*): No, sir, the manager is on a call at the moment.

   Angle. Mike and the clerk, Ford standing behind Mike.

CLERK: But, I assure you, we have *no* . . .

MIKE (*turning away from the desk*): That's alright. Thank you . . .

CLERK: I'm *very* sorry, sir . . . if . . .

MIKE (*walks away from the desk with Ford*): That's alright. (*To Ford; sotto:*) Did you see what I just did?

FORD: Yes.

Mike nods.

Interior: Elevator—Night

Ford and Mike.

FORD: What if he comes back?

MIKE: He had on a tuxedo. We would believe he's going out for the evening.

FORD: What if he does?

They get off the elevator.

Interior: Hotel Corridor—Night

Ford and Mike stepping off the elevator.

MIKE: If he does, we deal with *that* thing *then*. (*He holds up the room key.*) In or out . . . ?

Ford takes the key. He pulls her to him and kisses her passionately.

Interior: Hotel Room—Night

Ford and Mike getting dressed.

MIKE: We should be leaving.

FORD: You said he wasn't coming back.

MIKE: Probably not, but why should we wait for him.

HOUSE OF GAMES

PHOTO BY LOREY SEBASTIAN

PHOTO BY MICHAEL HAUSMAN

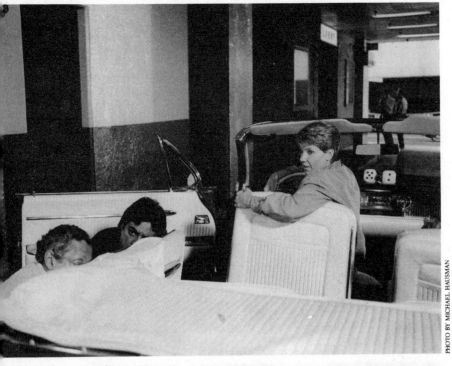

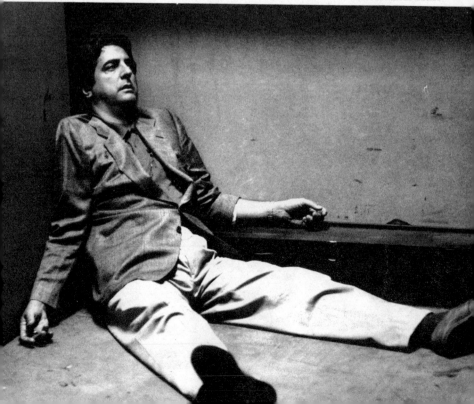

FORD: Some people would say you're an interesting man.

MIKE: I'm a con man, I'm a criminal. You don't have to delude yourself. You can call things what they are. You can call yourself what you are.

FORD: What am I?

MIKE: Listen to me, because there's lots of things in the world, and there's many sides to each of us: good blood, bad blood, and somehow all those parts have got to speak. The burden of responsibility's just become too great. It's true, isn't it . . . ?

FORD: Yes. It is.

MIKE: I know it is. I read this somewhere: if you're fired from your job, take something, take a pencil, something, to assert yourself, take something from life. And I think what draws you to me is this: I'm not afraid to stand up and assert myself, and I think *you* aren't, either.

FORD: Do you really think so . . . ?

MIKE: Yes. That's *exactly* what I think. I'm going to wash up, and then let's get out of this guy's room. (*Mike leaves the room.*)

Pause. Ford sighs, goes over to the dresser, picks up a comb, starts combing her hair, looks down at the dresser.

Angle—Point of view. Personal effects on the dresser. A pile of change, a small antique silver pocketknife. Some cigars.

Angle. Ford picks up the pocketknife. Looks at it. Takes it over to her pile of clothes and slips it into her pants pocket.

Interior: Hotel Lobby—Night

Ford and Mike walking out of the hotel lobby. Camera follows them out onto the street.

DOORMAN: Taxi . . . ?

MIKE (*to Ford; leans over and kisses her*): You gonna take a taxi home?

FORD: Where are you going?

MIKE: I've actually, got to be right *here* in . . . (*Checks his watch.*) Oh, *Christ* . . .

FORD: What *is* it?

MIKE (*quickly, worried*): Look, look, you remember Joey from last night? The . . .

FORD: Your friend . . .

MIKE: *Slowly* . . . look around, and tell me if you see him.

Ford looks around.

  Angle—Point of view. Across the street Joey and a businessman are walking down the street, slowly, conversing, as after a good meal.

  Angle. Ford and Mike.

FORD: Uh, *yes* . . . he's just crossing the . . . I don't under . . .

MIKE: Look . . . oh, Christ . . . (*He looks around.*)

FORD: What is it?

MIKE: There's a *bit* that I'm supposed to do here.

FORD: I'll do it with you.

MIKE: No. This is not "games," this is . . .

FORD: I'll do it with you. Just tell me what to . . .

Mike looks around.

MIKE: Aw, *hell* . . . Babe, you're fucken up my timing . . . (*Decides, he takes her arm. They start to walk toward the corner.*) *Come* on. You're my *wife.* You follow my cue. Whatever I do. Don't volunteer *anything.* However strange things seem, KEEP YOUR MOUTH SHUT. And the only one you know is *me.*

Angle. Ford and Mike walking toward the street corner. Joey and the businessman are approaching the same corner from the other side of the street. Both pairs arrive at the street corner at the same time. Also, another man, carrying a small suitcase, arrives at the corner, and hails a cab. This is the Vegas man from the card game at the House of Games. The Vegas man hails a cab, and we hear him say, "Airport, in a hurry" to the cab driver, as he gets in the cab. The cab drives away. But the Vegas man has forgotten his suitcase, which is left standing on the curb, just as the two pairs of people, Mike and Ford and Joey and the businessman, converge next to it, waiting for the traffic light to change. Pause.

JOEY (*to the group*): Ha. Fellow left his suitcase.

MIKE: I'm sorry . . . ?

JOEY: Fellow left his suitcase.

MIKE: Well, he probably came from the hotel. Let's, uh . . . let's take it back, and . . .

Mike leans down to pick up the suitcase. As he picks it up, the suitcase falls open revealing its contents to Mike and Ford. Ford gasps. Pause.

(*Softly:*) Holy Christ . . .

Angle—Point of view. The interior of the suitcase. It is full of stacks of hundred dollar bills.

Angle. The group. The businessman and Joey have crowded around, they are all looking awestruck at the case. Pause.

MIKE: Um . . . (*Pause.*) I think we should . . .

He starts to walk back to the hotel with the case.

JOEY: No, hold on, wherever you're going, *I'm* going *with* you . . .

BUSINESSMAN: That's for *goddamn* sure.

Interior: Businessman's Hotel Room—Night

The businessman is in his shirtsleeves, smoking. The suitcase is on the bed.

BUSINESSMAN: Now: look: look: look; this has *got* to be stolen money . . .

MIKE: How do we know that?

JOEY: What are you, fucking *nuts*? There's eighty thousand *dollars* in the goddamn bag. Who's going to be . . .

BUSINESSMAN: . . . that's right . . .

JOEY: . . . carrying that kind of money in a "bag" the middle of the *night* . . .

BUSINESSMAN: That's absolutely right . . .

JOEY: . . . and . . .

BUSINESSMAN: And there's no *goddamned* way I'm turning that money over . . .

JOEY: . . . why should we? So some "cops" can split it?

BUSINESSMAN: . . . that's absolutely right . . .

JOEY: I'm not going to do it, and I'm not going to let *you* do it.

BUSINESSMAN: Now, let's just stop fucking around here: this money fell into our *laps*—there's no way to give it *back* . . . and all of us *know* what we're going to do, so let's just face the goddamn *facts*, 'cause we're going to *split* the *money*. So let's just *do* it. (*Pause.*)

MIKE: I . . . uh . . . now . . . um . . . look. I . . . I . . . I work in a *bank* . . .

JOEY: I don't want to know your personal . . .

MIKE: Will you just shut up for a second. Listen to what I'm going to tell you: I work in a bank. *If* this money is clean . . . *If* it's clean, *if* it's not counterfeit . . . I say this: I say we *split* it. (*Pause.*) And we split it down the middle, and we walk away and this never happened.

BUSINESSMAN: . . . that's what *I* say.

MIKE: I . . . here's what I think we should do: I say that . . . we're going home tomorrow. I'll take the money to the bank, and . . .

JOEY (*laughs*): Are you *nuts* . . . do you think that we're *insane* . . . ?

MIKE: Listen to what I'm going to say: we keep it *intact* . . . we don't *touch* it. I check it out. *If* it's hot, we . . . we *sit* on it. For six months, a year . . .

JOEY: . . . and you have the money all this time.

MIKE: Listen to what I'm going to tell you . . . I'll . . . alright: I'll go to . . . I can go to a bank tomorrow morning. *Here.* In *Chicago* . . . and . . . I can get . . . I can get ten, twenty thousand dollars. Clean money. *My* money . . . I'll write a draft . . . you *keep* the money . . .

JOEY: . . . we keep *your* money . . . ?

MIKE: . . . yes . . .

BUSINESSMAN: *Wait* a second . . . wait a second . . . *back* up . . . back up: *I'll* go to a bank. Alright? *I'll* . . . (*To Joey:*) Eh?

Joey shrugs.

I'll give *you thirty* thousand dollars . . . and *I'll* get the thing checked out. I'll give you my money, and *I'll* keep the suitcase, you sonofabitch . . .

> *Angle—Close-up. Mike and Ford. Mike turns to Ford, nods slightly, sadly, meaning you see what human nature is?*

Interior: Hotel Room—Day

> *Angle—Insert. Mike's hand holding his own wristwatch. It reads 8:30.*

> *Angle. The hotel room. The suitcase is still on the bed. Mike is holding his wristwatch; he rubs his wrist and puts his watch back down on the bureau. Ford, Joey, and the businessman, also, seated around the room.*

BUSINESSMAN (*sighs*): I'm going to wash up, and then we'll go.

Mike nods.

JOEY (*to businessman*): Go. I'll keep a watch on the suitcase.

The businessman goes into the bathroom. We hear running water. Pause.

MIKE (*to Ford; sotto*): You got a little bit more than you *bargained* for, hey?

FORD (*waking up*): Hmmm. (*Beat.*) What's happening?

MIKE: Yeah.

FORD: I don't understand how this thing works.

MIKE: Well, alright, I'm going to tell you.

JOEY: Don't include the broad in it, Mike, for chrissakes, you had to drag her along, she don't have to know how we do this.

MIKE: Cool it, Joe, it's going good.

JOEY: Don't mouth it, it's going how it's going. You were a fool to've brought the broad.

MIKE: Be that as it may. (*To Ford:*) The mark gets dressed, we take him to the bank, he gets to ship the suitcase to himself in . . . where's he from . . . ?

JOEY: Baltimore.

MIKE: Baltimore. Before we let him do that, he gives up thirty thousand dollars. Before we ship it, we switch the suitcases on him, and we've got his thirty thousand dollars.

FORD: I don't get it, if it's phony money in the case, why do you have to switch it?

MIKE: Who said it was phony money? It's real. That's the beauty of the thing. We're showing the guy eighty thousand real dollars. We borrowed the money from the mob for one night, tonight we've got to pay it back.

JOEY: Okay, he's finishing up, let's take it to the Bank.

MIKE (*to Ford*): I hope you've enjoyed yourself. You have seen sights that few have seen.

JOEY: You were a fool to have brought the broad.

MIKE: It's *over*, Joe. (*To Ford:*) You did real good. (*Ford smiles.*) You better get your coat.

Ford nods, starts for the coat closet. Looks back at the businessman in the bathroom. Reflected in the door mirror she sees he is wearing a gun in a holster. He closes the door.

Ford walks to the door. Camera follows. Through the door she hears:

BUSINESSMAN (*voice over*): Coming out in about five minutes. Not as far as I can determine, negative, none of them are armed, we'll act as if they were in any case. When you come in . . . have the female officer go for the woman, get her down on the ground and *frisk her good*. I don't trust her. I'll take the young guy, and you take the old. The signal is I clear my throat. (*Pause.*) Say again . . . ? (*Holds the earpiece closer to his ears.*) Yes. At the bank.

   Angle—Close-up. Ford moves her head back, terrified.

   Angle. Ford comes back to Joey and Mike.

FORD (*sotto*): He's a cop.

MIKE: What?

FORD: He's a cop. I . . . he's . . . I heard him on the walkie-talkie.

Mike stands.

MIKE: Get out of here . . . you got to get *out* of here . . . get *clear.*

FORD (*terrified*): I . . . Yes. I *have* to . . . I . . .

MIKE: *Come* on . . .

He starts moving her toward the door. Camera pans to show Mike and Ford moving toward the door to the hall. As they do so, the businessman comes out of the bathroom and blocks their way.

BUSINESSMAN: Where you going . . . ?

MIKE: Well, it's just my *wife* . . . she's got to call the . . .

Mike starts opening the door.

BUSINESSMAN: No, no, no, hold *on* . . .

MIKE: *We're* going to stay with you, *she* . . .

The businessman blocks the door.

BUSINESSMAN: Nobody goes anyw . . .

MIKE (*starts to shove him aside*): She's very *ill* . . . she . . .

Mike shoulders the door open, Ford starts to squeeze through. The businessman draws a gun. Also pulls out his badge case and flips it open.

BUSINESSMAN: Police! *Don't move.* Get back or I'll blow your goddamned . . .

Ford and Mike are still trying to get through the door, all pushing the businessman. There is a shot. The businessman throws Mike out of the way and tries to prevent Ford from exiting the door. Pause. Ford and Mike step back. Pause. The businessman falls to the floor, splattered by blood. Pause. Mike kneels over him.

JOEY: How is . . .

MIKE: Yeah. He's dead . . . let's get the hell *out* of . . .

FORD: Oh, my god . . .

JOEY: Why did you have to kill him, are you out of your mind?

They all stand. Joey starts looking around the room, picking up any stuff he may have left.

MIKE: We've got about seconds to get out of here . . .

Mike holds open the door, Ford and Joey go through the room.

Interior: Staircase, Hotel—Day

In a succession of shots, we follow Ford, Mike, and Joey down the staircase, out into a service corridor on the ground floor.

Mike motions the others back, leans around a corner.

   Angle—Point of view. A policeman, standing guard out on the street.

   Angle. Ford, Mike, and Joey, in an alcove off the hotel garage.

MIKE: They're out there.

JOEY: She's killed us, man, the bitch has killed us dead.

In the background, the garage elevator opens, a vintage red Cadillac inside. Mike looks at the car.

MIKE (*to Ford*): Steal the car.

FORD: I can't do that.

Joey grabs Ford and hits her viciously in the face.

JOEY: Do you want to spend the rest of your life in jail, or do you want to steal the car?

MIKE (*to Ford*): They don't know you. We need you to steal the car.

Beat. Ford walks across to the car. Camera follows.

  Angle. Ford getting into the car. She starts the car. Pulls over to the two men. They get in the car, crouching in the backseat.

  Angle. Ford driving the car out of the garage, past the policeman.

Exterior: Desolated Area—Day

A deserted industrial area on a canal. The red Cadillac, Joey wiping down the interior with a rag. Ford and Mike in the background.

JOEY: All my life, Mike, all my life I never had a moment's violence. Never had a moment's violence.

MIKE: Forget it. Wipe it down and let's get out of here.

JOEY: And then you had to bring your squarejohn broad into it. You had to bring your trick into the game.

Joey takes the keys from the car and throws them into the canal.

MIKE: I brought the broad? What about the cop, where'd you get the cop?

JOEY: I found him at the apparel show, he looked like a businessman, he looked . . .

MIKE: Okay, okay, okay. Wipe it down. Let's get out of here.

　Angle. Ford and Mike.

MIKE: In a couple of minutes we're out of here, it's over, nobody even knows your name. We give the money back to the mob . . .

Pause. Mike turns to Joey.

　Angle. Joey, Mike and Ford, Joey standing, fixed, looking inside the car.

MIKE (*to Joey*): Where's the briefcase . . . ? You had it, you had it at the hotel.

Beat.

JOEY: It's not here.

MIKE: Where *is* it, Joe . . . ?

FORD: What does it mean?

MIKE: Where *is* it, Joe . . . ?

JOEY: I'm sorry, Mike, I was scared.

MIKE: You were scared? You sonofabitch, you've *killed* us . . .

JOEY: I'm sorry, Mike, when we were at the Hotel.

MIKE: SHUT UP. Let me think for a second . . .

FORD: WHAT DOES THIS MEAN?

MIKE: It means we lost eighty thousand dollars, and if we can't give it back tonight to the Mob, they'll turn us over for that cop we killed. (*To Joey:*) You got senile, old man . . .

FORD: I can give you the money.

MIKE: I need eighty thousand dollars by this evening.

FORD: I'll get it, I'll give it to you.

Beat.

MIKE: You have that kind of money?

FORD: I can get it.

Beat.

MIKE: Then, for god's sake, *get* it.

Interior: Taxicab—Day

Mike and Joey in the backseat.

MIKE: Funny how things happen sometime.

Joey turns to look out of the window.

> *Angle—Point of view. Ford coming out of a bank, carrying a large bag under her arm.*

Angle. Interior, the cab, Joey gets out, takes the bag, Ford gets in.

JOEY: I'll tell them . . .

MIKE: They know what happened, you don't have to tell them a goddamned thing. (*To driver:*) Start for the airport.

The car starts. Mike and Ford hold a whispered conversation in close-up.

FORD: What happens now?

MIKE: Joey gives the money back to the mob, and then he goes away. I'm going to go away. You're going to stay here because you have a life here. Listen to me: You're going to get a strong urge to confess. To thievery, to murder, you're going to want to confess. Don't do it. What happened was an accident. The fact you were there was an accident. So you go and forget it. I just wish . . .

He kisses her.

(*To driver:*) Stop the cab.

Angle. Exterior of the cab. The cab pulled over on the shoulder of a throughway on ramp. Ford gets out of the cab. The cab pulls into traffic.

Angle—Close-up. Ford watching the cab pull away.

Interior: College Hallway—Day

Maria, lecturing to a group of students. We hear nothing.

Angle. Ford, outside the lecture room, looking in. A late student moves past Ford to open the door. We hear Maria lecturing as the door opens.

MARIA: Compression, inversion, elaboration, are devices for transforming the latent into the manifest. In the dream, and also, in the . . . ? In the *Joke!*

As she makes her point she points her finger at the class, as if she held a gun. We hear a gunshot.

Angle—Close-up. Ford, recoiling.

Angle. The businessman's face.

Angle. Ford's hand, turning the pages of her notebook, to the page which reads "House of Games."

Angle. The businessman sliding down the wall. A loud bell rings.

Angle. Ford in the hall, stunned. The bell stops. We hear Maria calling "Maggie . . . Maggie, What is it . . . ?"

Angle. The hall. The students, changing classes. Maria, in the classroom door, calling to Ford.

FORD: I have to . . . I have to talk to you.

MARIA: What. *Anything.* (*Pause.*) What *is* it . . . ? (*Pause.*)

FORD: You know . . . you know the dream where . . . you've done something terrible . . . some . . . some . . . and you're . . . going to . . . *die,* or . . . you've *killed* someone . . . and you say: you say: "If Only This Was a Dream . . ." I've had dreams like this. What would I not give if this was a dream, and . . .

MARIA: Maggie. Darling. Come upstairs. Sit down and tell me. (*Takes her arm.*)

Ford breaks free.

FORD: No! Listen to me. No. What do you do? What do you do when . . . when . . . And if you reveal yourself you betray someone else, and . . .

MARIA: When you've done something "unforgivable." When you've done something unforgivable, you *forgive* yourself. Now, come upstairs and . . .

FORD: No.

MARIA: My God! Maggie, what's the trouble? My poor child. *Whatever* it is . . . there's nothing that doesn't have a second ch . . .

FORD: "It isn't as if I've *killed* someone . . ."

A student comes over and pulls Maria aside to ask a question. As she does so Ford pulls away. Walks out the door.

Interior: Ford's Office—Vestibule—Day

Ford, still clothed in the clothes of the night before, walks into her vestibule. A young woman patient rises from one of the chairs.

YOUNG WOMAN PATIENT: Dr. Ford . . . do I have the wrong day, am I . . . ?

FORD (*moving past her, opens the door to her inner office*): I'm very sorry. I'm very sorry. I'm quite ill. I'll have to . . .

YOUNG WOMAN PATIENT: . . . are you *alright* . . . ?

Ford brushes past her.

FORD: Didn't I just tell you. What did I just say . . . ?

Ford goes into the inner office. Camera follows. She closes the door behind her. Moves to the window shades. Draws them. Goes over and sits in her chair. Picks up the telephone.

(*On phone:*) No calls through . . . on any circumstances. Call my appointments for today and cancel them.

She hangs up the phone, she rubs her face. She takes out a ciga-rette and lights it. She shakes her head, closes her eyes. Starts to cry. She reaches down to her desktop.

Angle—Insert. Ford is picking up a copy of her book Driven.

Angle. She takes the book. Pause. She hurls it across the room.

Angle. The book hits a large framed diploma on the other side of the room. The glass shatters.

Angle. Ford walks over to the diploma, a medical degree in her name. She reaches through the fragments of glass and takes out the diploma. Crumples it. She looks down at her hand.

Angle—Point of view. Her hand is bleeding badly.

Angle. She goes to her desk. Opens the desk drawer. Looks down.

Angle—Point of view. Various objects in the desk drawer. A small package of Band-aids. She is bleeding all over the desk drawer. Trying to put on the Band-aid. She does so. Her hand stops.

Angle. Ford looking down in horror at something in the desk drawer. She picks it up.

Angle—Point of view. Ford holding the now-bloody pocketknife which she took from the black man's hotel room.

Angle. Ford holding the bloody pocketknife. Frightened. Throws it in her wastebasket. Thinks.

Ford takes all the artifacts, throws them in the wastebasket. She leans back, unbuttons her jacket, sighs. She looks down; her shirt, inside her jacket, is spattered with blood. She rips off her bloody shirt, throws it in the wastebasket.

Camera follows her across the room to a gymbag. She takes out a sweatshirt, puts it on. We hear a knock on the door.

Angle—Close-up. Ford turns to look at the door. The knock is repeated.

BILLY HAHN (*voice over*): Dr. Ford? Dr. Ford, it's Bill Hahn.

Angle: At the door. She opens it, to reveal Billy beyond.

FORD: What do you want?

BILLY: I called up to cancel. Your office said that you weren't taking any calls. I have to be away for a few days.

FORD: Yes. I think it's best if we suspended treatment for a while.

Beat.

BILLY: Are you alright?

FORD: Yes. Thank you.

Beat. Ford closes the door. Camera follows her to the waste-basket. She picks it up, starts out of the room.
Pause. She thinks of something. She hurries back to her desk. Takes her purse, rummages through it, takes out the datebook, takes out a folded piece of paper.

Angle—Insert. It is the check for six thousand dollars she wrote when she went to the House of Games the first time. Her fumbling hands put the check in an ashtray and set fire to it.

Angle. Ford watching the check burn. Pause. She rummages through her desk, pulls out a file.

Angle—Point of view. The file reads "Billy Hahn." Ford flips through the pages.
We see the page we have seen previously, which reads: "Compulsive succeeds in establishing a situation where he is out of control." And below it, written "The character of Mike, the 'Unbeatable Gambler.' Seen as omniscient, who 'doles out punishment' . . . HOUSE OF GAMES."
Her hands lay these pages aside. She digs deeper in the file, takes out the small nickeled automatic pistol she had taken from Billy. She pulls out another sheet. It is Billy's I.O.U.

Exterior: Ford's office building—Day

Ford comes out of the service door, carrying her wastebasket. She walks toward a dumpster. As she walks she sees something.

Angle—Point of view. Billy Hahn, hanging up a payphone across the street. Billy continues walking down the street. As he turns the corner we see the vintage red Cadillac. Billy gets into the car.

Angle. Ford at the dumpster, looking at Billy getting into the car.

Exterior: Charlie's Tavern—Night

The red Cadillac parked.

Angle. Ford, across the street, camera follows her across toward the tavern, and into the back door.

Interior: Charlie's—Night

Ford's moving point of view. A well-built black man, his back to camera, talking on the payphone in the back of the tavern.

Angle. Ford, sneaking into Charlie's through the back.

Angle—Point of view. In the front of the tavern, Billy Hahn having a drink with the Vegas man. Behind Ford the black man brushes past, and announces to a table: "I just won five thousand dollars in a baseball game." Ford turns to look at him.

Angle—Point of view. It is Mr. Dean. As he slides into a booth, the businessman/policeman gets out.

BUSINESSMAN: Why'nt you let me have a taste?

MR. DEAN: I'd let you have a taste, you weren't so goddamn *cheap* all the time.

BUSINESSMAN: How come I always got to play the straight guy . . . ?

MR. DEAN: *Think* about it.

MIKE (*voice over*): Who filled the goddamn water pistol . . . ?

JOEY (*voice over*): I did.

MIKE (*voice over*): Goddamn water pistol made a puddle big enough to swim in.

Angle. Ford, walking over toward their booth, shielded by a stack of beer cases.

Angle—Ford's point of view. Joey, Mike, Mr. Dean, the businessman, seated at the booth.

BUSINESSMAN: Well, it's what you pay for, it's realism.

The Vegas man comes over to the booth.

JOEY: Well, is she going to stand up?

VEGAS MAN: Well, like he said, she's On Tilt, but he thinks she'll stand up.

MIKE: Pay the kid off.

Joey takes some bills from Ford's bank bag, hands them to the Vegas man.

MIKE: Keep him a little scared.

VEGAS MAN (*takes the bills, starts off*): Oh yeah.

MR. DEAN: Mike: How'd you know she was going to go for it?

MIKE: Go for it, the broad's an *addict* . . .

JOEY: Oh. This is great. This is fantastic. Listen to this: we're dressing up the hotel room . . .

MR. DEAN: "My" hotel room . . . ?

MIKE: Yeah. We put some stuff, we put forty, fifty bucks up on the bureau . . .

MR. DEAN: Uh huh . . .

MIKE: Yeah, so it looks like somebody's in the room. Now: the broad steals my pocketknife.

BUSINESSMAN: No.

MIKE: My hand to God. She boosts my Lucky Pocketknife.

JOEY: The bitch is a booster.

MIKE: The bitch is a born thief, man, "Show me some con men . . ."

BUSINESSMAN: Well, we showed her some con men.

MIKE: We showed her some *Old* style . . .

MR. DEAN: Yessir . . .

MIKE: Some *Dinosaur* con men. Years from now, they'll have to go to a *museum*, see a frame like this.

MR. DEAN: Took her money, and screwed her, too.

MIKE: A small price to pay.

Angle—Close-up. Ford, recoiling. She leans back against the wall, her back to the booth.

BUSINESSMAN (*voice over*): Mike, you are the Ring-Tailed Rounder, you are King Kong.

MIKE (*voice over*): One Riot, one Ranger.

MR. DEAN (*voice over*): What's next?

MIKE (*voice over*): For me, a rest. I'm going to Vegas tonight on the ten o'clock. You want to come?

MR. DEAN (*voice over*): Nah, this time I'm quitting winners.

MIKE (*voice over*): Missing you. What did I say? We got the two hotel rooms. Speaking of which, three hundred dollars for a hotel room?

MR. DEAN (*voice over*): Always show a little front, Mike, you taught me that yourself.

MIKE (*voice over*): Oh, you're such a flatterer. Fifty-two ninety for the two policemen's uniforms, two hundred dollars that we gave the kid . . .

Interior: Airport—Night

A departures announcement TV screen. Announces three flights left, the final one is for Las Vegas, departing 10:00 p.m. The Las Vegas entry is joined by a blinking "Now Boarding" sign.

Angle. Ford, dressed for traveling, looking up at the screen. Checks her watch.

Angle—Insert. The watch reads 9:42.

Angle. Ford looking at her watch. Sees something.

Angle—Point of view. Mike, carrying a small suitcase, coming in from the street.

Angle. Ford takes a deep breath, moves toward him on an oblique angle. He sees her, stops, she "sees" him. She walks over to him.

FORD (*softly*): Mike . . . Mike . . . what are you . . . what are you here . . . ? We can't be here . . .

MIKE: What are you doing here . . . ?

Angle—Close-up.

FORD (*sotto*): Listen . . . listen . . . they're *following* me . . . they're *following* me . . .

MIKE (*sotto*): . . . they are?

FORD: Come on . . . we . . . we . . . we . . . we must keep moving . . .

She leads him outside. They come out of the building.

Angle. Ford and Mike.

MIKE: Look: we can't be seen together.

FORD: No. We must. Don't leave me . . .

MIKE: You're in no danger . . .

FORD (*simultaneous with "danger"*): I *told* you. They're *waiting* for me . . . there were *men* there. (*Pause.*) What are you doing here? I thought you . . . I thought you . . .

MIKE: I couldn't get on the right flight. Now: Look: If they haven't followed you here, then you have some time. We have to split up.

FORD: No. I can't . . .

MIKE: *Yes.*

FORD: No. I can't . . . how can I do it without *you*, we, this is a *godsend* that . . .

MIKE: I'm going to tell you where I'm going. Alright. Yes. We'll . . . you're right. We're going to take separate flights.

FORD: No. No. No. I'm so frightened. And . . . Mike: Mike: I . . . I took all my money. I took all my money out of the bank. I'm . . . and you'll help us disappear. We'll disappear together. Mike: I've got a quarter of a million dollars. We can live . . . we . . . I can't believe I'm seeing you . . .

Interior: Airport, Lower Floor

Mike and Ford by a bank of lockers. Ford opens a locker, takes out a small Gladstone bag.

MIKE: Do you think that you were followed?

FORD: I don't know. I'm frightened all the time.

MIKE: Yes.

He looks around, leads her down a corridor, camera follows.

FORD: I bought my ticket in another name.

MIKE: I think that's wise. ·

FORD: My real name is Margaret.

MIKE: Margaret. (*Beat.*) We're going to get you out of here. I promise you. We need a plan.

They stop outside a door to the baggage area. Mike tries the door, it is open. Camera follows them into the deserted baggage area. Mike leads Ford over to an unused conveyor belt. They sit.

FORD: It was fate I found you.

MIKE: Yes. It was.

FORD: Because, *together* . . .

MIKE: . . . Yes. We *can*.

FORD: And when I saw them . . . when I saw that they came *after* me . . .

MIKE: It's alright now. You're safe.

FORD: . . . I *knew*. That I was being *punished*.

MIKE: No. It was an *accident* . . . No . . .

FORD: No. I knew. That I was bad. Do you know why? Do you know when I knew? Because I took that knife.

MIKE: What knife?

FORD: Your pocket knife. From that hotel room. And I said, "That's why it happened. That's why it all . . ." Yes. Because I'm bad. (*Pause.*) Because I'm a *thief*. Because I'm . . . It's because I'm . . .

She sees something in him.

Angle—Ford's point of view. Mike.

(*Voice over:*) What is it . . . ?

Angle. Mike and Ford.

Mike, Mike: what is it?

Mike gets up, starts checking the baggage area slowly.

MIKE: Oh. You're a bad pony. N'I'm not going to *bet* on you. (*Pause.*)

FORD: I . . . ?

MIKE: You see: The thing of it is: You just said "*my* pocketknife." (*Pause.*)

He continues checking out the baggage area.

FORD: I . . . I don't underst . . .

MIKE: You said you took "My" pocketknife out of the hotel room.

FORD: I . . . ?

MIKE: You see, in my trade this is called, what you did, you "cracked-out-of-turn." Eh? You see? You crumbed the play. (*Pause.*) What do you want? (*Pause.*) What do you fucken *want* from me . . . ? You want your eighty *grand* back, I can't *give* it back. I split it up. What do you want? Revenge?

He sits down. Pause.

FORD: I gave you my trust.

MIKE (*laughs*): Of *course*, you gave me your trust. That's . . . you asked me what I *did* for a living . . . this is it. Look, look, I'm *sorry*. I'm sorry I "hurt" you. Really. You're a good kid, now, whatever it is that you feel that you have to do . . .

He starts for the door.

FORD: Sit down, please.

MIKE: I'd love to, but I . . .

FORD: I said to Sit Down:

MIKE: Whaddaya gonna do, go to the *Cops*?

FORD: I may.

MIKE: And tell them *what*? Whattayagonna tell 'em, Stud? That the author of the best-selling *Driven*, "A Guide to Compulsive Behavior," gave her cash away to some con man? (*Pause.*) You see my point? (*He starts to leave the baggage area.*) But we've had fun! You must say that.

FORD: I said sit *down*.

She takes the nickeled automatic pistol out of her pocket. Mike reaches for the doorknob.

If you walk out that door I'm going to kill you.

MIKE: I don't believe you.

FORD: What is life without adventure? (*She chambers a round and points the pistol at him. Pause.*)

Mike lets go of the doorknob. He sits down. Pause. He shrugs.

MIKE: What . . . ? (*Pause.*) What do you want?

FORD: You took my money.

MIKE: How naughty of me.

FORD: You raped me.

MIKE: Is that what I did . . . ?

FORD: You took me under false pretenses.

MIKE: Golly. Margaret. Well, that's just what "happened," then, *isn't* it? *Okay:* Look: You got "Stung," and you're "Hurt." *I* can understand that. You're *stuck* 'n you're steaming . . .

FORD: I want to know how you could do what you did to me.

MIKE: It wasn't *personal.* Okay? And, really, funny as that sounds, I'm sorry that it happened. But it *did,* and we've all got to live in an imperfect world. (*He gets up.*)

FORD: You used me.

MIKE: I "used" you. I did. I'm *sorry.* And you learned some *things* about yourself that you'd rather not know. I'm sorry for that, too. You say I Acted Atrociously. Yes. I did. I do it for a living. (*He gives her a salute and starts for the door.*)

FORD: You sit down.

MIKE: I'd love to, but I've got some things to do.

She cocks the gun.

(*Of gun:*) You can't bluff someone who's not paying attention.

Ford shoots him. He falls.

Are you *nuts*? What are you . . . *nuts* . . . ?

FORD: I want you to beg me.

MIKE: Fuck *you*. I'm not going to beg you for a goddamn *thing*.

FORD: Beg me.

MIKE: S's a goddamn bluff. You're *all* bluff. Whataya, gonna *kill* me? and then go to Jail? Give up that good *shit* that you have, that "Doctor" stuff, that "money," your "car". . .

FORD: It's not my pistol, I was never here. (*She shoots him again.*) Beg for your life. Or I'm going to kill you.

MIKE: Hey, no.

FORD: I can't help it—"I'm out of control."

MIKE: Hey, no. Oh . . . I . . .

FORD: Beg me for your life.

MIKE (*coughing*): Hey, fuck *you*. This is what you always *wanted*—you crooked bitch . . . you *thief* . . . this is what you always . . . (*He starts to cough blood.*) You always need to get caught—'cause you know you're bad . . . live with *this*. I never hurt anybody. *I* never shot anybody . . . you're gonna . . . you're gonna . . . you're gonna . . . you sought this out . . .

We hear a jet revving up and starting its take-off.

This is what you always wanted. I knew it the first time you came in. You're worthless, you know it. You're a whore. I knew you the first time you came in. You came back like a dog to its own vomit. You sought it out.

Ford shoots him again.

"Thank you, sir, may I have another?"

Ford shoots him three times. As a jet thunders by overhead. Ford walks slowly to retrieve her bag, leaves the room. Pause. Silence.

Interior: Restaurant—Day

An open greenhousey restaurant. Ford, tanned, dressed lightly, at the bar, holding a drink. She looks around. A man accosts her.

MAN: Are you Dr. Margaret Ford? (*Pause.*) Are you Dr. Margaret Ford?

FORD: Yes. I am.

MAN: Would you sign my book . . . ?

The man produces a copy of the book, hands it over to Ford. Ford takes it, takes a pen, begins to write.

> *Angle—Insert. Ford writing on the title page: "Forgive yourself." As she finishes writing, we hear someone calling her "Maggie."*
>
> *Angle. Ford finishes with the book. The call is repeated. She looks for the source.*

Angle—Point of view. Maria standing in the restaurant doorway beckoning to Ford.

Angle. Ford goes over to Maria. They embrace.

MARIA: Oh, darling. I've missed you. How *are* you?

FORD: I'm fine. Really fine.

MARIA: Are you?

FORD: Yes. I absolutely am.

Camera follows them. to a table in the dining room. They sit.

MARIA: Do you know how frightened I was for you? Before your trip?

FORD: . . . it was just the strain . . . what with the book coming out . . .

MARIA: No, no, I know. But there was something . . . *something* . . . Something on your *mind* . . .

FORD: That's right—and you said, when you've done something unforgiveable, forgive yourself, and that's what I've done, and it's *done.*

MARIA: Good. What are we going to eat? What did you eat down there?

A waitress comes to the table.

WAITRESS: Dr. Littauer?

MARIA: Yes?

WAITRESS: You're wanted on the phone.

Maria sighs. Gets up.

MARIA (*over her shoulder*): I'm sorry, darling. Order for me.

Ford is left alone at the table. She looks around the restaurant. The woman at the table backing up theirs is lighting a cigarette with a gold lighter. She and Ford nod slightly at each other. Pause.

The woman replaces the gold lighter in her purse. Ford looks down at the menu, puts the menu down.

Ford turns to the woman.

FORD: Excuse me . . . ?

WOMAN WITH LIGHTER: Yes?

FORD: Could you tell me what that is on the buffet?

The woman turns to look at the buffet. As she does so, Ford reaches across toward her purse.

Angle—Insert. Ford's hand taking the gold lighter out of the woman's purse.

Angle. The woman, turning back, Ford, sitting at her table.

WOMAN: A Waldorf salad.

FORD: Thank you.

Angle. Ford's hands under the table, holding the lighter.

Angle. Ford at the table, her hands come up with the lighter, she lights a cigarette, and then holds the lighter covered in her hands. She smiles.

Selected Plays & Screenplays
Available from Grove Weidenfeld

___ GUERN	0-8021-5122-1	Arrabal, Fernando GUERNICA AND OTHER PLAYS	$17.50
___ ABSURD	0-8021-3157-3	Ayckbourn, Alan THREE PLAYS (Absurd Person Singular; Absent Friends; Bedroom Farce)	$9.95
___ CASCA	0-8021-5099-3	Beckett, Samuel CASCANDO	$8.95
___ ENDGA	0-8021-5024-1	Beckett, Samuel ENDGAME and ACT WITHOUT WORDS	$4.95
___ ENDS	0-8021-5046-2	Beckett, Samuel ENDS AND ODDS	$8.95
___ KRAPP	0-8021-5134-5	Beckett, Samuel KRAPP'S LAST TAPE	$7.95
___ GODOT	0-8021-3034-8	Beckett, Samuel WAITING FOR GODOT	$5.95
___ BEHAN	0-8021-3070-4	Behan, Brendan THE COMPLETE PLAYS (The Hostage; The Quare Fellow; Richard's Cork Leg)	$9.95
___ KVETC	0-8021-3001-1	Berkoff, Steven KVETCH and ACAPULCO	$6.95
___ BAAL	0-8021-3159-X	Brecht, Bertolt BAAL, A MAN'S A MAN, and THE ELEPHANT CALF	$8.95
___ CAUCA	0-8021-5146-9	Brecht, Bertolt THE CAUCASIAN CHALK CIRCLE	$5.95
___ GALIL	0-8021-3059-3	Brecht, Bertolt GALILEO	$5.95
___ GOOD	0-8021-5148-5	Brecht, Bertolt THE GOOD WOMAN OF SETZUAN	$4.50
___ JUNGL	0-8021-5149-3	Brecht, Bertolt THE JUNGLE OF THE CITIES	$9.95
___ 3PENNY	0-8021-5039-X	Brecht, Bertolt THREEPENNY OPERA	$4.95
___ CHERR	0-8021-3002-X	Chekhov, Anton THE CHERRY ORCHARD	$8.95
___ NINE	0-8021-5032-2	Clurman, Harold (ed.) NINE PLAYS OF THE MODERN THEATRE (Waiting for Godot; The Visit; Tango; The Caucasian Chalk Circle; The Balcony; Rhinoceros; American Buffalo; The Birthday Party; Rosencrantz & Guildenstern Are Dead)	$16.95
___ 3BYCOW	0-8021-5108-6	Coward, Noel THREE PLAYS (Private Lives; Hay Fever; Blithe Spirit)	$9.95
___ LAUGH	0-8021-3130-1	Durang, Christopher LAUGHING WILD and BABY WITH THE BATHWATER	$7.95
___ BETBOO	0-394-62347-9	Durang, Christopher THE MARRIAGE OF BETTE AND BOO	$7.95
___ PHYSI	0-8021-5088-8	Durrenmatt, Friedrich THE PHYSICISTS	$6.95
___ COUSI	0-8021-3152-2	Foote, Horton COUSINS and THE DEATH OF PAPA	$8.95
___ TOKILL	0-8021-3125-5	Foote, Horton TO KILL A MOCKINGBIRD, TRIP TO BOUNTIFUL, TENDER MERCIES	$10.95
___ RAPPA	0-8021-3044-5	Gardner, Herb I'M NOT RAPPAPORT	$7.95
___ BALCO	0-8021-5034-9	Genet, Jean THE BALCONY	$8.95
___ EASTE	0-8021-3174-3	Greenberg, Richard EASTERN STANDARD	$9.95
___ SECRE	0-8021-3175-1	Hare, David THE SECRET RAPTURE	$8.95
___ LARGO	0-8021-5163-9	Havel, Vaclav LARGO DESOLATO	$7.95
___ TEMPT	0-8021-3100-X	Havel, Vaclav TEMPTATION	$9.95
___ INGE	0-8021-5065-9	Inge, William FOUR PLAYS (Come Back Little Sheba; Picnic; Bus Stop; The Dark At the Top of the Stairs)	$9.95
___ BALD	0-8021-3079-8	Ionesco, Eugene FOUR PLAYS (Bald Soprano; The Lesson; Jack or Submission; The Chairs)	$8.95
___ RHINO	0-8021-3098-4	Ionesco, Eugene RHINOCEROS AND OTHER PLAYS	$7.95
___ EXITKI	0-8021-5110-8	Ionesco, Eugene THREE PLAYS (Exit the King; The Killer; Macbett)	$12.95
___ UBUPLA	0-8021-5010-1	Jarry, Alfred THE UBU PLAYS	$9.95
___ AUREV	0-8021-3114-X	Malle, Louis AU REVOIR LES ENFANTS	$6.95
___ 5TV	0-8021-3171-9	Mamet, David FIVE TELEVISION PLAYS	$12.95
___ GLENG	0-8021-3091-7	Mamet, David GLENGARRY GLEN ROSS	$6.95
___ GAMES	0-8021-3028-3	Mamet, David HOUSE OF GAMES	$5.95
___ LIFETH	0-8021-5067-5	Mamet, David A LIFE IN THE THEATRE	$9.95

Selections from Grove Weidenfeld (continued)

___ SPEED	0-8021-3046-1	Mamet, David SPEED-THE-PLOW	$7.95
___ CLOCK	0-8021-3127-1	Miller, Arthur THE AMERICAN CLOCK and THE ARCHBISHOP'S CEILING	$8.95
___ DANGER	0-8021-5176-0	Miller, Arthur DANGER: MEMORY	$5.95
___ ODETS	0-8021-5060-8	Odets, Clifford SIX PLAYS (Waiting for Lefty; Awake and Sing; Golden Boy; Rocket to the Moon; Till the Day I Die; Paradise Lost)	$10.95
___ ORTON	0-8021-3039-9	Orton, Joe THE COMPLETE PLAYS (The Ruffian on the Stairs; The Good and Faithful Servant; The Erpingham Camp; Funeral Games; Loot; What the Butler Saw; Entertaining Mr. Sloane)	$10.95
___ CARET	0-8021-5087-X	Pinter, Harold THE CARETAKER and THE DUMB WAITER	$7.95
___ MOUNT	0-8021-3168-9	Pinter, Harold MOUNTAIN LANGUAGE	$6.95
___ PROUS	0-8021-5191-4	Pinter, Harold THE PROUST SCREENPLAY	$3.95
___ ELEPHM	0-8021-3041-0	Pomerance, Bernard THE ELEPHANT MAN	$6.95
___ HURLY	0-8021-5097-7	Rabe, David HURLYBURLY	$7.95
___ BOOM	0-8021-5194-9	Rabe, David IN THE BOOM BOOM ROOM	$8.95
___ AUNT	0-8021-5103-5	Shawn, Wallace AUNT DAN AND LEMON	$8.95
___ ANDRE	0-8021-3063-1	Shawn, Wallace MY DINNER WITH ANDRE	$7.95
___ EVERY	0-8021-5045-4	Stoppard, Tom EVERY GOOD BOY DESERVES FAVOR and PROFESSIONAL FOUL	$3.95
___ REAL	0-8021-5205-8	Stoppard, Tom THE REAL INSPECTOR HOUND and AFTER MARGRITE	$7.95
___ ROSEN	0-8021-3033-X	Stoppard, Tom ROSENCRANTZ & GUILDENSTERN ARE DEAD	$6.95
___ TRAVE	0-8021-5089-6	Stoppard, Tom TRAVESTIES	$4.95
___ NOPLAY	0-8021-5206-6	Waley, Arthur (trans.) NO PLAYS OF JAPAN	$9.95
___ COLOR	0-8021-3048-8	Wolfe, George C. THE COLORED MUSEUM	$7.95

TO ORDER DIRECTLY FROM GROVE WEIDENFELD:

YES! Please send me the books selected above.

Telephone orders—credit card only: 1-800-937-5557.

Mail orders: Please include $1.50 postage and handling, plus $.50 for each additional book, or credit card information requested below.

Send to: Grove Weidenfeld
IPS
1113 Heil Quaker Boulevard
P.O. Box 7001
La Vergne, TN 37086-7001

☐ I have enclosed $_____ (check or money order only)

☐ Please charge my Visa/MasterCard card account (circle one).

Card Number_____

Expiration Date_____

Signature_____

Name_____

Address_____ Apt. _____

City_____ State _____ Zip _____

Please allow 4–6 weeks for delivery.
Please note that prices are subject to change without notice.
For additional information, catalogues or bulk sales inquiries, please call 1-800-937-5557.   ADCD